beth moore

blessed mornings & restful nights

devotions to begin and end
your day in God's presence

Blessed Mornings & Restful Nights

introduction

I would consider it a treat, if it were possible, to sit and talk with you about the Lord and His great love for you. To be able to share a time together, perhaps over a cup of coffee and our Bibles opened is something I would treasure. But more important than being in each other's presence is the time we carve out of our day to be in God's presence. I believe it's a priority that pays the greatest dividend to our day.

In this devotional, I share from my heart on real-life issues. My life and ministry are an open book – affording me the opportunity to tell you how great God is in redeeming lives for His Kingdom purpose. Every morning and night, you will find a scripture and thought about our walk with the Lord. I pray they will speak to your heart and, if not specifically for you, prepare you to touch someone else's life with hope and encouragement. That's what we find *every time we make time* to be in God's presence.

God bless you as you read **Blessed Mornings & Restful Nights.** Over the next 90 days, may you find my words uplifting and encouraging, and God's Word from Psalm 16:11 fulfilled in you – *You make known to me the path of life; you will fill me with joy in your presence, with eternal pleasures at your right hand.*

DAY 1

the kindness
of God

morning

I led them with cords of human kindness, with ties of love; To them I was like one who lifts a little child to the cheek, and I bent down to feed them. Hosea 11:4

Did you know that God is a philanthropist? He is the lover of mankind. The worldly culture is trying to deny God, but confess philanthropy. I want you to understand that any desire man has to do something out of love for humanity is coming from the image of God, whether or not He is ever acknowledged.

Kindness already has a savior. It is Jesus Christ. I don't know what God is calling you to do in kindness to somebody else today, but it is not to become their savior. Be kind by pointing them continually to the One and only Who holds that authority.

evening

*When our fathers were in Egypt, they gave no thought
to your miracles; they did not remember your many
kindnesses, and they rebelled by the sea, the Red Sea.*
Psalm 106:7 NIV 1984

As you wind down from your day, remember: kindness has a good memory. Most rebellion is caught up
in forgetfulness. When we go off in a rebellious tangent
we have forgotten that God has been kind to us! God
has been kind to us even when we were ungrateful and
pursuing everything we could in sin. There is a kind
heart in you because Jesus Christ put it there. Let's open
our mouths with wisdom and let the law of kindness be
upon our tongues.

I will remember Your kindnesses to me, O Lord.

shame is no longer your burden

 morning

O my God, in you I trust; let me not be put to shame;
let not my enemies exult over me. Psalm 25:2 ESV

The strategy of your spiritual enemy is to keep you from looking up. Shame is one of his greatest weapons; it will keep you looking down. Jesus, on the other hand, constantly desires to reveal Himself to us. He so wants to show us that He is at work in our lives. If we are bound by shame and looking down, or looking in, we're going to miss Him. Today, Jesus once again longs to reveal Himself in all manner of ways, through His Word, through your circumstances, and through people He places in your life.

What is your spiritual posture today? Are you carrying a burden that was not meant for you to carry? When you feel heavy hearted, ask Jesus to reveal Himself to you. Look for Him in every circumstance. You will not be disappointed, for He is with you!

evening

"I have not come to call the righteous but sinners to repentance." Luke 5:32

Be ready to combat shame with the Word of God. We can be delivered from the sin and still be in the shame because we've trusted God for only half the work – to forgive us **but not to deliver us.** Satan takes great joy in reminding us of our sin, but we do not have to listen. Silence the enemy by declaring God's Word in every area of your life. Sleep in peace tonight and wake up refreshed, guilt-free and full of life.

Jesus, You have set me free, and You continue to set me free, from shame!

He's calling you

 morning

....

Simon Peter said, "I'm going fishing." John 21:3–6 NLT

If you know Jesus, you have a calling on your life.

Scripture tells us that before the foundation of the world, God already knew and had ordained in advance His calling on your life. That is why He put you in this particular generation. It's why you are here on planet earth, *at exactly this time* – because your calling fits with what is going on in your sphere of influence.

What you need to understand is that most of us don't do our calling professionally. For most, life requires us to work a job outside of our calling to support our ministry. I do want you to know that there's a connection between the two: There are things that God is teaching you in your work place that are very strategic in your calling. Ask Him to show up at work! Ask Him to give you spiritual eyes to see, ears to hear, and to make you aware of Him – even if you are in what you may think is the most Godforsaken workplace you have ever entered! Listen, He is *with* you today.

☀ evening

....

Do not be like them, for your Father knows what you need before you ask him. Matthew 6:8

Let Jesus confirm His call on your sweet life. He calls you by name. The most important relationship in your life is the one between you and the Lord Jesus Christ. Let everything else go! Listen, He knows our hearts toward our families. If we're married, He knows our hearts toward our spouses. He knows what we want for our children. For just a little while, before you go to sleep tonight, let every other concern in life go and just push pause for a moment. Thank Him that He knows you by name and knows every need before you ask, and that He cares.

I'm thankful I'm called by God and my life has purpose. I want to always be open to Your leading, Lord.

fill me up, Lord!

morning

*Satisfy us in the morning with your steadfast love, that
we may rejoice and be glad all our days.*
Psalm 90:14 ESV

Every one of us has an innate, overwhelming desire to be
loved. Our lives don't just need to be full of things or the
activities of life, we need to be full of somebody's love.
If we are not feeling properly loved, we will seek to find
something else to fill us.

But the Word of God teaches us how to come to Him.
Before He fills me up, I've got to empty myself out. I
confess my sin and shortcomings and bring Him my
concerns and all that weighs me down. You have no idea
how dangerous you would be if you would live filled to
the measure with the fullness of Christ. You can start
today, and every day being satisfied in your spirit that
God loves you and will be with you today.

◉ evening

....

*Now to him who is able to do immeasurably more
than all we ask or imagine, according to His power at
work within us . . .* Ephesians 3:20

God wants to fill us with His Spirit continuously. The
filling of the spirit is not about a spiritual gift, it's about a
state of being full! And with that fullness comes power,
and you never know what you're going to do with that
kind of power; certainly something beyond yourself. We
serve an overflowing God of love Who loves when we
share the overflow with others.

**May Your love flow through me, Lord. I pray for an
overflow of love so I can be a blessing to others.**

DAY 5

an issue of the heart

morning

If anyone says, "I love God," and hates his brother, he is a liar; for he who does not love his brother whom he has seen cannot love God whom he has not seen.
1 John 4:20 ESV

Our hearts are home to love or hate. Of course God is always calling us to love, but the reality of life is that hate can creep in. If you are dealing with a hate issue in your life, here is what I see to be the big problem. It takes up so much space in our hearts. It's easy to tell ourselves, "I'm saving my hatred for one specific relationship." But the truth is hatred will suck all of the love out of us. Hatred kills relationships, security, our sense of well-being and our sense of peace. Hatred will definitely kill a family.

Don't harbor hatred. Begin today by asking the Lord to reveal to you any hatred you might hold in your heart. Hatred only hinders your happiness and scars those around you. You cannot imagine the feeling that awaits you when you replace the hatred with love.

☀ evening

Create in me a clean heart, O God, and renew a right spirit within me. Psalm 51:10 ESV

Whatever root of hatred you have carried, God wants to restore that relationship. He wants to wipe away every ounce of remaining guilt and shame and replace that space with love and forgiveness. Just as the father ran to his prodigal son and remembered his past no more, this is your Father's heart for you – and His desire in all of your relationships. Love awaits your pursuit of the Father's heart.

That's my prayer tonight, Lord – to have a clean, loving, peaceful and restored heart.

keep watchful!

 morning

Mine eyes are ever toward the LORD; for he shall pluck my feet out of the net. Psalm 25:15 KJV

I love the word "pluck" here. The use of this word in the scripture is so great! He's not just going to grab us out, not just going to lift us out; He's going to pluck us out!

When the Word of God sheds light on an area of need in our lives, an area of bondage, it always comes with a prescription for what we can do with it. We are never hopeless. Once we get into God's Word, and God brings us out, we begin to learn the pattern of what comes right before we are about to get captivated by something we end up hating. We will begin to be able to look into a situation and say, "I see you. I see you!" Keep your eyes on the Lord and His Word, and be watchful.

☽ evening

To you, O LORD, I lift up my soul. O my God, in you I trust; let me not be put to shame; let not my enemies exult over me. Psalm 25:1–2 ESV

You may know you are caught in a net. Anything that gets us trapped and hooked into it is, indeed, a net. A net is meant to surprise; you don't spread a net out in full view. If the enemy is going to have a net set for you or me, it's going to be camouflaged.

The Word of God is our key to seeing Satan's nets. Whatever your need may be, I want you to set aside any guilt and anxiety you have over it and simply ask God to deliver you. We serve an awesome, delivering God Who looks out for His own!

I'm so glad You are for me, God! My heart is *for* You!

DAY 7

your tongue is a tell-all!

 morning

She openeth her mouth with wisdom; and in her tongue is the law of kindness. Proverbs 31:26 KJV

What is it to live by the law of kindness? This scripture underscores a character trait to be admired and sought out. Here, a son is being told what kind of wife to find. You want a home filled with the law of kindness and with wisdom. Sooner or later, what we bury in our heart will spill out of our mouths. When we speak, we have a choice about how to express ourselves, and our tongue is ultimately a tell-all! Make kind words a part of your day and watch as God uses your words and wisdom to be a blessing to others. It takes supernatural power to stay kind in the mean world that we are living in.

evening

Even before a word is on my tongue, behold, O LORD, you know it altogether. Psalm 139:4 ESV

Many of us are natural-born talkers, some may be more talkative than others. Sometimes you have to taste something to know whether you really want to make a meal out of it. You need to taste kindness as it comes out of your mouth. I trust that the Holy Spirit will convince you as you read God's Word that kind words and actions are something to be sought after in a life grounded in wisdom.

May my words be kind, my actions loving and my life reflect the wisdom of the Word.

you're family!

 morning

··

"I will tell of your name to my brothers; in the midst of the congregation I will sing your praise." And again, "I will put my trust in him." And again, "Behold, I and the children God has given me." Hebrews 2:12–13 ESV

You may need to know today that Jesus Christ is not ashamed to call you His sister or bother. Even after all you've been through, after all you've done, if you will trust Him for that redemption, trust Him for that healing and trust Him to bring meaning out of that disaster, He will show you that He has never been ashamed of you.

The time has come to receive your dignity back. This is the day of your deliverance. This is the day when He comes to bring us beauty out of our ashes. This is the day we can have our honor back.

☀ evening

Unless the LORD builds the house, its builders labor in vain. Unless the LORD watches over the city, the watchmen stand guard in vain. Psalm 127:1 NIV 1984

Isn't it a beautiful thing that Jesus is a carpenter by trade? Because no matter how the winds and the storms have come to tear your house down, Jesus Christ can rebuild it if you let Him. The Word of God says that we are being built into a spiritual house of living stones. If He can bring a stone back to life, He can bring you back to life also.

I will gladly give You the pieces of my life so You can complete Your work in me!

you weren't created for isolation

 morning

··

A father to the fatherless, a defender of widows, is God in his holy dwelling. Psalm 68:5 NIV 1984

Do you long for a family or for God to restore your family? Any family can be restored if everybody is willing, but, sometimes all parties may not be. We have a psychological need for people in our lives that we love like family and who love us like family. One of the things I'm seeing today in the body of Christ is an invasive loneliness that people cannot quite put their finger on. I'm here to tell you that God can add to your family.

evening

God sets the lonely in families, he leads forth the prisoners with singing; but the rebellious live in a sun-scorched land. Psalm 68:6 NIV 1984

No matter what kind of prison you've been in, no matter what kind of bondage has gripped you, or what has held you captive, if you're willing, God can heal your broken heart and set you free. If we choose to rebel against the power of God and His ability to put us back together again, the Scripture says it's like living in a sun-scorched land. You feel the heat, and life is a dry and desert-like experience. But, His love will always reach out to you, longing to help you and give you a life of peace and blessing.

May I never rebel against Your love, O God. I open the doors of my heart and ask You to do Your will in me.

DAY 10

rest in life for the rest of your life!

morning

"Come to me, all you who are weary and burdened, and I will give you rest." Matthew 11:28 NIV 1984

Do you long for inner, heart healing? Sometimes we fear what it might take to cooperate with God for healing, thinking it is going to hurt so badly we will never survive it. This is one of the biggest lies the enemy tells us. We end up living with the pain day in and day out and never letting God bring us to freedom because we're afraid of what it would take. Can I encourage you not to carry the pain any longer? Perhaps this is a word for a friend you will see today. Jesus, our Healer, offers rest from the pain of life. Give it to Him today. Let this be a day of healing.

˙⭑●⭑ evening

....

O LORD my God, I cried to you for help, and you have healed me. Psalm 30:2 ESV

Like a jammed toe, or finger, that is out of place, every now and then we have to let God grab hold of our prolems and reset our lives. Just like the pain, it may be intense for a moment but it is part of getting to the other side and that's when healing comes. Don't be afraid to be made whole!

I don't know what your day consisted of, but right now take a deep breath and thank God for His ability to heal broken hearts and bad memories. This can be the day when you decide to gather the courage and do what it takes to know the powerful healing of God. Let's pray to that end.

I rise in the morning to greet You with praise and rest each night because You are faithful.

DAY 11

beating the shame game

morning

He heals the brokenhearted and binds up their wounds. Psalm 147:3

Shame can come in many ways. Sexual abuse has become a much more talked about reason, but shame can come in all sorts of ways. We can feel shamed by ridiculous things like 15 extra pounds, or an old, broken down car we drive, or where we live. If Christ came to do anything at all, He came to deliver us from our shame. Today, God is saying to all who have ears to hear, "Let Me in. I'll take the pain and help remove the shame. It's one more gift I long to give you."

Today's scripture is a word of hope the world needs to hear . . . and you can be the messenger.

·*●·* evening

....

*When I consider your heavens, the work of your
fingers, the moon and the stars, which you have set in
place, what is mankind that you are mindful of them,
human beings that you care for them?* Psalm 8:3–4

Grace is unmerited favor. The grace of God comes freely
to the undeserving. Sometimes we have a fear that somehow we will betray a person we lost by getting healing
and wholeness for ourselves. But this is what Christ came
to do! Even if relationships do not heal, a marriage never
comes back together, a sibling is never restored to you, a
best friend of so many years is never restored back again,
YOU get to be restored! I pray that God has a miracle in
mind for you and that whatever you've gone through,
God will restore you.

God, I praise You for the countless works of restoration You have completed, and others in progress,
including mine.

you have your Father's heart!

 morning

But love your enemies, do good to them, and lend to them without expecting to get anything back. Then your reward will be great, and you will be sons of the Most High, because he is kind to the ungrateful and wicked. Luke 6:35

This scripture is saying we never resemble our Father in heaven more than when we love someone that is hard to love. Think of people in your life right now that are ungrateful and live in a state of feeling sorry for themselves, constantly throwing pity parties that no one wants to attend. So often we fall into the trap of believing that to be kind to that person, we are giving them power over us. What we don't realize is the power is in the kindness. We are never more like our Father in heaven than when we are kind to the ungrateful and the wicked.

☾ evening

Be merciful, just as your Father is merciful. Luke 6:36

The third chapter of 2 Timothy brings something very interesting to light. It says in the last days there will be perilous times, but it doesn't talk about the environment or circumstances. Scripture tells us that the further and further you and I get on the kingdom calendar, the meaner people will get. Like Christ, we must love them and respond in kindness. Perhaps we heard it when we were children, but there is a command still bugging us to no end: love your enemies – not just those that are easy to love.

Father, give me Your eyes to see the tears of others, ears to hear their cries and Your heart to reach out and touch them in their time of need.

hold your head high

 morning

You made him a little lower than the heavenly beings and crowned him with glory and honor.
Psalm 8:5 NIV 1984

When shame comes, when brokenness, devastation or calamity come your way, very often it will result in the feeling of a loss of dignity. I want you to know that God can give that back to you. God is the One Who gives us back our honor. God is the one that gives us back our dignity. He has it; you never lost it, it has always been in His hands; it still is His possession and His right to give. Walk with your head held high today. You are a child of God. You are loved, forgiven and destined for purpose.

✦● evening

....

O LORD, our Lord, how majestic is your name in all the earth! You have set your glory above the heavens. From the lips of children and infants you have ordained praise because of your enemies, to silence the foe and the avenger. Psalm 8:1–2 NIV 1984

The only thing that makes the devil shut his mouth is praise for God. Open your mouth and begin to praise. Speak up! Sing with all of your heart and with every bit of the capacity in your lungs and you will silence the foe, the avenger. Praise your Savior for Who He is and all that He has done for you. Praise Him for restoring your dignity and honor.

As the scripture also says, *With my mouth will I make known thy faithfulness . . .* **Psalm 89:1**

redeemed!

 morning

....

For he says, "In the time of my favor I heard you, and in the day of salvation I helped you." I tell you, now is the time of God's favor, now is the day of salvation.
2 Corinthians 6:2 NIV 1984

God can redeem (turn around, restore) even the worst day of your life! He can go back, pick that thing up and bring such a transformation and redemption that the devil will be sorry he ever messed with you!

Ask the Lord to redeem you, ask Him to transform you and start looking forward to today. "Now" is a key word in your scripture today. We serve a "now" God Who is able to deliver you!

⦿ evening

"My grace is sufficient for you, for my power is made perfect in weakness." Therefore I will boast all the more gladly of my weaknesses, so that the power of Christ may rest upon me. 2 Corinthians 12:9 ESV

I would love for the enemy to have to think about that when he tempts my perpetrator to come against me and abuse me. It reminds him of his worst memory, because I started something that day that did not turn out well for him. I made a decision. There comes a time when you must draw a line in the sand spiritually. Are you just going to let him get away with torment? At some point you must stand up and say, "Enough!" When the enemy tries to render us powerless, God comes to us and says, "My power will be made perfect in your weakness. I will show you what I can do. I will defy every single odd. Trust in me."

If God is for me – and He *is* **—I can overcome every torment and accusation the enemy throws at me. His grace is sufficient for me!**

discipline is not a dirty word

 morning

"For the Lord disciplines the one he loves, and chastises every son whom he receives." Hebrews 12:6 ESV

If you are like me, you can look back on situations where unfortunate circumstances and calamities came partially from my poor decisions. When we are going through a time of consequences, we need to keep ourselves close to God . . . not run the other way. Only God can discipline us in such a way that will bring healing. He doesn't give us what our sins deserve. He only brings about the kind of chastisements (corrections) that have the capability to teach us. The goal of every chastisement of God is that the lame would not be disabled, but would be healed.

☀ evening

....

*For the moment all discipline seems painful rather
than pleasant, but later it yields the peaceful fruit of
righteousness to those who have been trained by it.*
Hebrews 12:11 ESV

Be encouraged as your day ends and rest in knowing that
the Lord knows every single thing you're dealing with.
He knows every single emotion, every single memory
that this is triggering and He is bringing those things to
the surface. This is not so you can feel pained by it, or be
reminded by it, but rather to help heal you! He lets things
come to the surface so that He can skim them off.

**God, as You look into the secret places of my heart
may Your light and love do the work necessary to
make me whole.**

heavenly handiwork

morning

The thief comes only to steal and kill and destroy. I came that they may have life and have it abundantly.
John 10:10 ESV

Anything God does, the enemy is going to attempt to counterfeit. God's desire is to bring us to such a place that our lives become a living testimony to His handiwork. He wants to remove every other excuse, every other reason for how far you have come, except that He is God and that He Himself did it. But you have an enemy; someone who is scheming to take down not only you, but your entire family. He is the enemy of every single institution God has built up and ordained. Know that he is vicious and relentless. Do not give him a foothold in your life, or in your family's life. I love the reminder of Proverbs 18:10 – God is your source for everything in life, a "strong tower" the righteous run to in time of need.

● evening

Then King David went in and sat before the LORD,
and he said: "Who am I, O Sovereign LORD, and what
is my family, that you have brought me this far?"
2 Samuel 7:18 NIV 1984

Let's close out today with prayer . . .

Father, I bless Your name and tell You again, "I want ears to hear You." Circumcise my heart so that I can feel my emotions toward You. And Father, where there is pain and where there is brokenness I pray that You would come in and tend to it. Father, even as an adult, every now and then I wish I had someone to mother me and father me. I know that You are my Father Who cares for me more than I can comprehend. You have set up this whole design called "family." And with everything in us we cry out, "Abba Father." Come and tend to the brokenness. Come and give me insight. Come and give me healing, Father. I ask this to bring glory to Your great name. And it is in the name of Jesus I pray. Amen.

I will live for You – through joy or sacrifice, misunderstanding or miracles. You are worthy of all praise, and my life is a witness to Your grace.

first rule in relationships

 morning

Rather, speaking the truth in love, we are to grow up in every way into him who is the head, into Christ . . .
Ephesians 4:15 ESV

Do you have any relationships in your life where you know you are called to stay friends, but already discern something is wrong? The Lord isn't necessarily telling you to run, but you are discerning something is not what it seems, a warning in your spirit, beyond emotion. Whatever the reason, as in any relationship, we must be able to speak the truth in love. If your relationship cannot survive you speaking the truth in love, you probably don't need to be in it. And most importantly, guard your heart. Ask the Lord to show you His purpose in that relationship.

☀ evening

The pride of your heart has deceived you, you who live in the clefts of the rock, in your lofty dwelling, who say in your heart, "Who will bring me down to the ground?" Obadiah 1:3 ESV

We should strive to be humble people in all of our relationships. Sometimes in life we can get a little "full of ourselves," and when we do that we are operating like mere men or women. The pride of our hearts will deceive us, and when there is arrogance we cannot trust our discernment. There will be too much "self" in the picture to see the truth.

God, help me to reflect Your love, Your patience and Your wisdom in all my relationships. May I glorify You and not me.

the daily adventure

 morning

Count it all joy, my brothers, when you meet trials of various kinds, for you know that the testing of your faith produces steadfastness. And let steadfastness have its full effect, that you may be perfect and complete, lacking in nothing. James 1:2–4 ESV

I have people tell me continually, "I find church boring." Well, guess what! You may have found a boring church, but you don't have a boring God. There is nothing boring about God! I want to live a life compelled by the love of Christ instead of seeking the comforts of this earth. When they lay me to rest, I want to have lived an adventure with Him. It doesn't take going to another country – it's simply being willing to get down on your knees and look in the face of someone you know is hurting so badly. The vulnerability of that face-to-face encounter is sometimes more than we can handle unless we are driven by the love of Christ. Today is one more day on your adventure in a world of great need. His love in you can make a difference – and that is never boring!

✶ ● ✶ evening

....

*Even though I walk through the valley of the shadow
of death, I fear no evil; for You are with me; Your rod
and Your staff, they comfort me.* Psalm 23:4 NASB

Do you realize what is at stake when we live motivated
by the comforts of this world? It will be one relational
rut after another, or a life of addiction trying to fill a void
only God's purpose in you completes. The real tragedy is
that we are going to miss the adventures of our calling.
For in that pursuit, we will find the comfort of Christ that
our hearts desire.

God, help me to think outside the "comfort zone"
and use me to be a blessing to others. Help me
look at my life through eyes of faith.

a watchful, discerning heart

 morning

And it is my prayer that your love may abound more and more, with knowledge and all discernment, so that you may approve what is excellent, and so be pure and blameless for the day of Christ.
Philippians 1:9–10 ESV

You've got to have a smart heart. We are called to love people, but be smart in your love. There can be times when we are called to minister to someone and you feel in your spirit a need to keep your guard up. Something might not be ringing true as you listen, but hang in there. You can know that God has called you to that person, but love them smartly and intelligently. Love with *knowledge* and *a depth of insight* so that you may be able to *discern*. Most importantly, ask the Lord to help you discern as you minister to them.

evening

Therefore do not pronounce judgment before the time, before the Lord comes, who will bring to light the things now hidden in darkness and will disclose the purposes of the heart. Then each one will receive his commendation from God. 1 Corinthians 4:5 ESV

You might be asking yourself, "How does a discerning person differ from a judgmental person?" God's Word tells us we are not to judge one another; however, we can definitely judge circumstances and situations. Often if we will just listen to people, and be sensitive to their needs, we will gain a much greater understanding of where they are in life. Usually the problem that is so evident is the result of something deeper. We need ears to really hear, and eyes to really see.

Lord, help me love others, and as I love, learn to discern. Help me to hear Your heart for others and not judge their hearts.

pursuing a life in the Spirit

 morning

For everyone who lives on milk is unskilled in the word of righteousness, since he is a child. But solid food is for the mature, for those who have their powers of discernment trained by constant practice to distinguish good from evil. Hebrews 5:13–14 ESV

The Word of God says that the more we mature, the more we are going to find that we have to distinguish between good and evil. The devil is not going to come out and appear before us in all his vileness. Who in the world would choose to follow him when he is in that state? That is why he had to become the beautiful, beautiful creature in the garden that could tempt Adam and Eve so easily. Of course, his strategy worked and they had to leave behind the beautiful life of fellowship that God had planned for them. God's Word is our guide to discerning all the good from all of the evil in our world today. There is no substitute for a time with God's Word every day.

☀ evening

....

But I say, walk by the Spirit, and you will not gratify the desires of the flesh. Galatians 5:16 ESV

We have to come to a place in this age of seduction, where we must be able to distinguish between good and evil. It's not easy and certainly not clear. But God will tell us if we seek Him. We've got to walk in the Spirit. What you and I will find is that we are never going to live a single day in the Spirit accidentally. If you end up living a life in the Spirit, it will not be because you just happened to; you will pursue a life in the Spirit.

I want a heart that is sensitive to Your ways, Lord. You are the light to my path and that still, small voice in my spirit. That is the voice I want to hear most of all.

examine yourself

 morning

"Do not judge by appearances, but judge with right judgment." John 7:24 ESV

There are four questions to ask yourself when it comes to discernment. If you come to a situation where you have some red flags, before proceeding, ask yourself the following questions:

1) Am I a critical or suspicious person by nature?
2) Am I jealous or do I feel threatened?
3) Do I have anything selfish to gain from being right about what I feel?
4) Are my emotions clouding my discernment?

If your answer to all four questions is no, then there is a good chance your red flag, your discomfort in your spirit, is valid.

☾ evening

For the word of God is living and active, sharper than any two-edged sword, piercing to the division of soul and of spirit, of joints and of marrow, and discerning the thoughts and intentions of the heart.
Hebrews 4:12 ESV

There are so many wonderful things we could be doing, so many wonderful things to give your time. Often I'm really excited about an opportunity when I first hear of it. But we've only got this one life God has given us, along with a calling, and in your service to Him there are seasons. What God has taught me to do through the years is wait until that initial emotional charge begins to wane and see if I still feel like it is something I'm supposed to do. I've learned to wait, sleep on it and let some time pass.

Take your time for important decisions in life . . . the bigger the decision, the more time and more prayer!

Help me to not rush into life decisions, Lord. Your Word, Your voice and the peace You've promised those who trust in You will guide me.

surrender again today

 morning

....

May have strength to comprehend with all the saints
what is the breadth and length and height and depth,
and to know the love of Christ that surpasses knowl-
edge, that you may be filled with all the fullness of
God. Ephesians 3:18–19 ESV

How many bad relational decisions have we made because of a deluded heart? All things we switch out for what Christ came to give us are idols. The Word of God tells us that, above all, the heart is deceitful. If we're just going to go through life on emotion and feelings, especially before we get sanctified (learning to live in righteousness) we're just an accident waiting to happen. We need to come before Christ and say to Him, "All right Lord, I am in need, waiting to be filled." That takes a heart of surrender.

evening

So we have come to know and to believe the love that God has for us. God is love, and whoever abides in love abides in God, and God abides in him.
1 John 4:16 ESV

We don't just need to be full, we need to be full of somebody's love. Every single one of us has an innate need to be loved. Where better to find the fulfillment we seek than to begin with God's love for us? He created us, accepts us as we are and longs to lavish His love on us. The Word of God is teaching us how to come to Him. Pour out your heart to Him again and again, surrendering to Him. God longs to fill you with His Spirit.

I receive God's love tonight and stand on this scripture – seeking to know His love and believe in His love for me.

Jesus is on to you!

 morning

But when Simon Peter saw it, he fell down at Jesus' knees, saying, "Depart from me, for I am a sinful man, O Lord." For he and all who were with him were astonished at the catch of fish that they had taken, and so also were James and John, sons of Zebedee, who were partners with Simon. And Jesus said to Simon, "Do not be afraid; from now on you will be catching men." And when they had brought their boats to land, they left everything and followed him.
Luke 5:8–11 ESV

You will never sin so much that you can keep Jesus away from you. Now, some people try to stay in their sin so He will leave them alone. But, it doesn't matter how many times you tell Him to go away, once He's on to you, He's *on* to you! You'll think that you're going to leave Him at home and then He shows up on the "boat!" Jesus loves a fisherman! Jesus loves a hairdresser, a bank teller, a teacher, a nurse, a doctor, a lawyer . . . He loves "whosoever will come." Enjoy your day with Jesus . . . wherever you go He goes, too!

● evening

....

Walk in wisdom toward outsiders, making the best use of the time. Colossians 4:5 ESV

Has God ever done something profound for you and after your initial delight, it hit you how well He knew you? I am often amazed at the scriptures God has me read and the circumstances surrounding the divine appointments He brings my way. This is the adventure of walking with Christ that I love to share with others; these are times when walking with God is anything but boring. I encourage you to pray and ask the Lord to bring you divine appointments. Prepare to be awed!

I'm glad You are a personal God Who calls me by name and has divine appointments prepared especially for me.

it only takes one

 morning

....

*Since, therefore, we have now been justified by his
blood, much more shall we be saved by him from the
wrath of God. For if while we were enemies we were
reconciled to God by the death of his Son, much more,
now that we are reconciled, shall we be saved by his
life.* Romans 5:9–10 ESV

Here is a question for you to think about. What if we're
throwing a fit in the midst of a "storm," when we are the
ones called to be the agent of favor to the others who are
caught in the storm? It just takes one person doing what
is right for God to bless a whole household, a workplace,
a community, or even a nation. As believers, we are a
perfect testimony to this truth. In the New Covenant all
were delivered because one person – Jesus Christ – was
on board with God's mission.

Don't limit your thinking of what God can do in your
life – submit each day to His will.

evening

He said to him, "Behold, I grant you this favor also, that I will not overthrow the city of which you have spoken. Genesis 19:21 ESV

As you walk faithfully with God, there are many people receiving a blessing because you are in their life. I'm not talking about salvation; each person has to come to salvation on their own, but there are people in your life who are definitely getting blessed because of your commitment to Christ. The enemy will constantly tempt us to turn and run; but remember, you are the key to blessing others. Stand firm in your faith and see the salvation of the Lord.

One life changed the world . . . and my life, through Christ, will change my world.

DAY 25

thankful for the storms in life ... really

morning

Consider it pure joy, my brothers, whenever you face trials of many kinds, because you know that the testing of your faith produces perseverance. James 1:2

Sometimes God allows us to be in a terrible storm in which the ship breaks to pieces. At first, we are distressed by the calamity all around us. Then, on the other side of the situation, we realize that we are in one piece and our faith is built up with strength and power in His Spirit. We see that what was broken to pieces was the devil and not us! Suddenly, we are thankful for the storms! It's wonderful to gain that perspective, but you have to ride out the storm to get to the "other side."

evening

As for you, you meant evil against me, but God meant it for good, to bring it about that many people should be kept alive, as they are today. Genesis 50:20 ESV

There is more purpose in the storms than you can even begin to realize. God can use a storm to bring you out of an addiction or a destructive relationship. You could be delivered from an area of unforgiveness or an unhealthy dependency could lose its hold. Ultimately, it's the enemy who will be broken to pieces – his work in you. Everything he tried to do to make you stumble or fall will come right back on him. Are you in a storm? Cling to the Lord!

Lord, You are my shelter in the storm, the rock on which I stand, and my Deliverer. I will fix my gaze on You.

constantly overcoming

 morning

"I have said these things to you, that in me you may have peace. In the world you will have tribulation. But take heart; I have overcome the world."
John 16:33 ESV

Constant suspense. Think about that phrase and think about the emotions and feelings that are associated with those words. Tribulations and trials can put you in a state of constant suspense. I believe God uses a *season* of continual suspense because it draws you closer to Him and more dependent on the Holy Spirit. But, when you are in a *duration* of suspense it can eat you up on the inside; not to mention your character, marriage, family and all sorts of relationships. Ask the Lord to show you where constant suspense is affecting you the most. Remind yourself that you are an overcomer in Christ.

evening

When hard pressed, I cried to the Lord; he brought me into a spacious place. The Lord is with me; I will not be afraid. What can mere mortals do to me? The Lord is with me; he is my helper. I look in triumph on my enemies. Psalm 118:5–7

I may have times of constant suspense, but I've got far more certainties.

1) I have constant certainty that the Lord is for me, not against me.
2) I have constant certainty that the Lord made Himself of no reputation and took on the form of a servant.
3) I have a constant certainty that when I cry to the Lord, He will answer me by setting me free.

What certainty in Christ would you add to this list?

Lord, may I rest in Your completed work on the cross, truly see You as my Savior and receive the peace You promised to all who believe in You.

you were not saved to be sour!

morning

"By this all people will know that you are my disciples, if you have love for one another." John 13:35 ESV

What are people thinking when they believe in order to be spiritual they have to be unlikable? Can't the gospel be shared by people who others want to be around, for a change? Yes, I understand that you have to be willing to be unliked in the face of standing up for your faith, or sharing Christ and being rejected. But, spiritual people do not have to be disliked by the world; in fact, it should be the exact opposite! How do you relate with those around you who do not know Jesus?

Let your light shine today, but, let your personality blossom, too. You don't have to be a people-pleaser, just a people-lover.

☀ evening

"You are the salt of the earth, but if salt has lost its taste, how shall its saltiness be restored? It is no longer good for anything except to be thrown out and trampled under people's feet." Matthew 5:13 ESV

To grow in favor with God and man is a really pretty thing. We do not want to just live for other peoples' approval, but we should have enough social skills in the power of the Spirit to relate to people in such a way that they find the gospel palatable. We are that salt and that light. We are the seasoning on that "plate of food" being presented called the gospel. We are to have the favor of God on us with people that do not know Him so that they are drawn to Him.

Help me to reflect Your love and be seasoning that adds to the flavor of life.

is it time to let go?

 morning

....

"Remember not the former things, nor consider the things of old. Behold, I am doing a new thing; now it springs forth, do you not perceive it? I will make a way in the wilderness and rivers in the desert."
Isaiah 43:18–19 ESV

Sometimes the message we're dealing with in life is, "Cut it loose!" Maybe it's a wonderful hobby or a job we are supposed to let go. Maybe it's time to move to a new city, or time to make some new friends. Maybe it's time to find a new church. Whatever it may be . . . cut it loose. We often hold to the familiar and fail to venture where God is prompting. He is a God of new things and knows where He is leading you. Move where God is leading and cut loose what is no longer of Him.

evening

Boldly and without hindrance he preached the kingdom of God and taught about the Lord Jesus Christ. Acts 28:31 NIV 1984

God doesn't deliver leftovers. He gives a fresh word, and delivers fresh starts. The Holy Spirit will move in our life when He is unhindered. Let nothing hinder God's work in your life. Perhaps we need to cut the rope of co-dependency or let go of our little "lifeboats;" those are the false things that we often look to for security. But, they can never fully save us in the storms of life, because they are not of God. Open up to the Holy Spirit's work in your life; God's unhindered work.

Release me, Lord, from my past; from those things that control my mind and heart. I want nothing to hinder my love for You, and what You have called me to do.

don't just settle

 morning

When a gentle south wind began to blow, they thought they had obtained what they wanted; so they weighed anchor and sailed along the shore of Crete.
Acts 27:13 NIV 1984

Discovery is a wonderful part of our spiritual walk. There are times we really think we have obtained what we want and yet, God still has something for us to discover. He will let some winds blow and collide right where we are standing in order to bring us to a place where we long for more of Him. There is a whole world of relationship to be had in Christ Jesus, far beyond anything this human realm could ever give us; we only think we have obtained what we really want. Ask the Lord to show you where you are settling for less than His best.

☀ evening

This phrase, "Yet once more," indicates the removal of things that are shaken – that is, things that have been made – in order that the things that cannot be shaken may remain. Hebrews 12:27 ESV

Within our materialistic society, we talk so often about a desire for too much when, spiritually and scripturally speaking, sometimes we are satisfied with way too little! Then, along comes a storm that blows everything out of place. We really do have an unseen enemy and power-ful foes in invisible places, and this really is a war. We tell ourselves that the enemy would not have the gall to hit us when we're down, but that is exactly when he will attack. As the book of Hebrews says, to shake everything that can be shaken so that which cannot be shaken will stand. It will stand!

I press on to discover all God has for me and remind myself He has much more in store . . . if I will only pursue His path for me.

the "perfect" storm

 morning

Blessed is the man who remains steadfast under trial, for when he has stood the test he will receive the crown of life, which God has promised to those who love him. James 1:12 ESV

The word "perfect" is a very interesting word in the Bible. In the New Testament, perfect doesn't always mean within context to be flawless or sinless, even though that is our concept of it concerning Christ and His plan for us. "Teleios" is the same as "perfect" in the Greek language and it means *to bring something to its goal or to its fulfillment.* Sometimes God allows storms to come together in such a way that they ultimately fulfill something that would never have happened otherwise. As hard as it is to see in the midst of the wind and the waves, there really is a plan in place . . . and what we do in the storm determines whether the storm is destructive or perfect.

☀ evening

Why do you see the speck that is in your brother's eye, but do not notice the log that is in your own eye? Matthew 7:3 ESV

The blame game always results in losing. It's all too easy in the midst of problems to place some kind of blame or fault on someone else closely involved. While we emphasize the faults in others, we don't see everybody's finger is pointed our way. The question of fault feeds the fury of every storm. Pray diligently for the Lord to bring the truth to light, to help you examine your own heart and live in peace. As Paul wrote to the Romans, *If it is possible, as far as it depends on you, live at peace with everyone.* (Romans 12:18 NIV).

God, help me to examine my heart through Your Word and use me to be a healer in life, a helper and not a fault finder.

a daily dose of drama

 morning

For I know the plans I have for you, declares the LORD, plans for welfare and not for evil, to give you a future and a hope. Jeremiah 29:11 ESV

We are going to have a great deal of drama in our lives. You might come face to face with some today. Drama is simply a part of the human experience on planet Earth. Now, picture God smack dab in the middle of your day and think about what kind of adventure you could have with Him. Think about your day with the perspective I'm about to share with you. Understand that God is not just trying to make us comfortable, but He is giving us a great story worth telling – that changes everything! Ultimately, your story has been conceived and is being played out to bring Him glory! All the people in our lives, even the villains, have a great impact in our story lines.

● evening

··

Jesus Christ is the same yesterday and today and for-ever. Hebrews 13:8 ESV

The only thing you can know for certain is that God remains the same in a world of change and obstacles you might not see coming. If you can learn to accept the unexpected, it keeps life exciting. We find a lot of security in same-ness, especially in terms of womanhood. A woman's idea of feeling secure is based on knowing that tomorrow there will be more of the same, and the week after that, too! While God may lead us on a path that has twists and turns, He is there every step of the way.

I will rest tonight knowing I don't know it all, but my God does, and He has promised me a future and a hope.

DAY 32

taking a stand

 morning

Like a muddied spring or a polluted fountain is a righteous man who gives way before the wicked.
Proverbs 25:26 ESV

We live in a world of messages proliferated by television and, especially, the internet. Honestly, most of it is not worthy of our time and attention. Amid the flood of information that comes our way, there is a level of crudeness that has crept into our culture and continues to rise. By remaining quiet, we simply become part of the crudeness by accepting it as our lot. The question many ask is, "What can we do that will make a difference?" I believe we can make a whole lot of noise – not even so much with our words, but with a life that reflects godliness, integrity and modesty. When we join together shoulder-to-shoulder for what is right, for what is dignity for humanity, there is victory. We take a stand and fight for humanity that does not yet know our Savior.

☀ evening

Do not be conformed to this world, but be trans-
formed by the renewal of your mind, that by testing
you may discern what is the will of God, what is good
and acceptable and perfect. Romans 12:2 ESV

There is so much beauty in God's creation of male and female – masculine and feminine. Our culture seems bent on blurring the lines. In addition to the crudities of conversation that you hear around you each day, many women especially seem to think, "If you can't beat 'em, join 'em," and lower their standards to fit in. God calls us to modesty, which becomes an increasingly conscious choice. We must heed the call of modesty in our character, in our heart and in our purpose. Guard your heart and protect the beauty of who God created you to be; do not let the world define you.

I am fearfully and wonderfully made. May I keep my heart pure and my mind renewed in God's Word for all of my life.

learning His leading

 morning

Because a great door for effective work has opened to me, and there are many who oppose me.
1 Corinthians 16:9 NIV 1984

Opposition does not mean you are heading in a direction that is not of God. Opposition can be something that arises because we are *absolutely on* the path of God's will for our lives. Opposition is in no way an indicator that you should stop or slow down; this is where spiritual discernment is vital. We cannot make assumptions based upon the quality of the life around us and the acceptance of our peers to determine where God wants us. What are you sensing in your spirit? Remember, we walk by faith, not by sight. You can be in the greatest spiritual battle of your life, and still have the peace of God ruling in your heart.

☽ evening

....

. . . knowing this first of all, that no prophecy of Scripture comes from someone's own interpretation. For no prophecy was ever produced by the will of man, but men spoke from God as they were carried along by the Holy Spirit. 2 Peter 1:20–21 ESV

Do you ever feel stuck in a certain season of life? We never want to get into a place where we are stagnant – not listening and waiting for the Lord to move. The Israelites learned to follow the cloud by day and fire by night (Exodus 13:21), but we have something more personal: the anointing of God. When the Spirit of the Lord moves on our heart we must stay attentive. In this world, there are a million messages a day vying for our attention. The Holy Spirit will not shout over them, so learn to quiet down and hear the most important voice in life – His.

Heavenly Father, I am thankful for the leading of Your Spirit. I ask that Your Word, Your voice and Your anointing direct my paths.

DAY 34

have you had your Word today?

 morning

We destroy arguments and every lofty opinion raised against the knowledge of God, and take every thought captive to obey Christ . . . 2 Corinthians 10:5 ESV

When was the last time you believed something you shouldn't have? What did you accept as truth that you later regretted or perhaps were even shamed by it? Life appears established, and we want to believe it's black and white. There are plenty of gray areas, and it's in these "gray zones" where we have the biggest capacity to get sideswiped. The truth is we live in a state of constant spiritual warfare, but here is your key to a successful life in the Spirit: You most accurately discern the Holy Spirit when you have an operating knowledge of God's Word. Have you had your Word today?

☀ evening

The natural person does not accept the things of the Spirit of God, for they are folly to him, and he is not able to understand them because they are spiritually discerned. 1 Corinthians 2:14 ESV

There is no substitute for God's Word in the life of a believer. We don't have to be Bible scholars, knowing all there is to know in 66 books of the Bible. The more we get to know God through His Word, the more we are going to be accurate when it comes to matters of spiritual discernment. Why? Because the Holy Spirit will never work contrary to God's Word; it was God-breathed. He will always be in *harmony* with what He has already given us. It will always line up.

Thank You for Your Word that brings me guidance, comfort, inspiration and encouragement. My heart's desire is to know Your voice.

DAY 35

revelation . . . today

 morning

···

Yet among the mature we do impart wisdom,
although it is not a wisdom of this age or of the rulers
of this age, who are doomed to pass away. But we
impart a secret and hidden wisdom of God, *which*
God decreed before the ages for our glory.
1 Corinthians 2:6–7 ESV

Today provides another opportunity to receive a fresh understanding of what God is doing in your life. The scripture today tells us there is godly wisdom being revealed – wisdom not of this world. The word "apoka-lupto" in the Greek language means to unveil something that was hidden. In the English language, we would call that "revelation": something the Holy Spirit wants us to understand, a hidden truth that is disclosed to us. God always has a fresh word for those whose heart is set on Him. Are you open for a fresh revelation today?

●* evening

. . . these things God has revealed to us through the Spirit. For the Spirit searches everything, even the depths of God. 1 Corinthians 2:10 ESV

One of the most revolutionary statements we will ever see in all of Scripture is *that we have the mind of Christ* (1 Corinthians 2:16). We have the ability through the spirit of Christ, and the activated mind of Christ in us, to know what we could not possibly know in human terms. I want you to remember God wants to speak to you, direct your paths and He has given you the mind of Christ to understand spiritual leading and discernment.

God, give me ears to hear Your voice and a heart after You, and thank You for the mind of Christ in me.

DAY 36

the Holy Spirit's presence in you

morning

But the Helper, the Holy Spirit, whom the Father will send in my name, he will teach you all things and bring to your remembrance all that I have said to you.
John 14:26 ESV

In thinking back to your moment of salvation, maybe you did not necessarily feel a thing. Maybe you did not feel any different physically than you did previously. Maybe it took days to really come to an understanding of what Christ had begun to do in you in that moment, but we are told, and it is a *spiritual fact*. In that moment, the Spirit of Christ takes up residence in us. The Holy Spirit literally lives within our vessel. You have a supernatural Teacher, Comforter and Guide living within you and that makes life exciting!

● evening

....

Since we live by the Spirit, let us keep in step with the Spirit. Galatians 5:25

We are on a journey. We are to walk in step with God. If we allow the Holy Spirit to be active in our lives; if we yield to the authority of Christ, then when we come to a crossroad we will know whether to go to the right or the left. You've been called of God and have a purpose here on Earth. Learn to listen to the voice of the Spirit and stay in the Word. And if the enemy says you can't possibly know God's voice, be reminded of Jesus' words in John 10:27. Jesus said, *"My sheep listen to my voice; I know them, and they follow me."*

Holy Spirit, I welcome Your direction in my life and thank You for speaking to me and through me to those You bring into my life for ministry.

DAY 37

drama or God adventure?

morning

No unbelief made him waver concerning the promise of God, but he grew strong in his faith as he gave glory to God, fully convinced that God was able to do what he had promised. Romans 4:20–21 ESV

If you go to a church, if you are married, dating, or have a friend, most all of us with a heartbeat live with drama of some sort. Life has a whole lot of drama. It is up to you whether or not you will turn that drama into a God adventure – something divine. You can have a story with drama, with nail biting, with crises of faith, with joys and sorrows, and opportunities that will come to say, "Will God come through for me this time or not?" I've got a good word for you today: *"Of course He will!"*

evening

Anyone who listens to the word but does not do what it says is like someone who looks at his face in a mirror and, after looking at himself, goes away and immediately forgets what he looks like. James 1:23–24

Your faith is more important to God than all your acts of righteousness. I promise that you can look all over the scriptures and it will tell you that faith is credited as righteousness. If you want to go from the pit to steady living, it will require action. It will require believing God concerning your identity in Him. When we believe God about whom He says He is and about whom He says we are, we will begin living differently. That's when our decisions change and our whole thought process is altered. Begin and end your day with faith in God.

My faith – trust, reliance, belief – is in You, God. You are my Creator and the Author and Finisher of my faith.

DAY 38

lean on Him
. . . learn of Him

 morning

. . . but test everything; hold fast what is good. Abstain from every form of evil. 1 Thessalonians 5:21–22 ESV

If you have the Holy Spirit of the living Christ dwelling in you, empowering you, and you have access to the complete Word of God – Genesis to Revelation – you can actually discern your own errors. We can make a judgment about something, walk away from it and think, "I'm getting a check in my spirit. Something is wrong." The leadership of the Holy Spirit within us is far greater than any human instinct, and He will lead you again today. Be sensitive.

·*●·* evening

....

For this people's heart has become calloused; they hardly hear with their ears, and they have closed their eyes. Otherwise they might see with their eyes, hear with their ears, understand with their hearts and turn, and I would heal them. Matthew 13:15

God is saying, "I don't want you to just see, I want you to perceive. I don't want you to just hear, I want you to understand. I want you to know and be able to see and be able to experience what is beyond just the natural before you. I don't want just your eyesight, I want your vision . . . perception . . . understanding." Then He says, "you will be healed." God is always at work, but it's not always obvious. Seek understanding and trust Him in all your ways.

God, I believe You are at work in all things in my life and I will trust in You. Help me to see with spiritual eyes and hear with spiritual ears to understand Your ways.

a lesson learned the hard way

 morning

But who can discern their own errors? Psalm 19:12

What would it be like to be able to discern the plan of God and the next move for our lives through His Spirit? I wonder how many of us can look back over the course of our lives and think, "You know, only God could have told me to do that." Before we look at the times we have done the wrong thing and missed the discernment or missed the warning, I want you to just think back on the course of your life about the times you got it right. A discerning spirit can be one of your greatest assets in life.

⬤ evening

. . . though he fall, he shall not be cast headlong, for the Lord upholds his hand. Psalm 37:24 ESV

You know a lesson learned is still learned even if you learn it the hard way. And sometimes a lesson sticks with us better and longer if we experience it in a difficult way. I completely blew it recently, and my mistake caused the Word of God to leap off the page at me. God began to teach me something totally new. I've recalled my mistake and thought to myself, "God allowed me that very walk so that He could capture my attention and teach me something very valuable for my life." Like the song says, "In the good times, praise His name. In the bad times, do the same."

Even when life seems bad, You are good, You are faithful and I'm glad You are holding my hand.

how is your comfort level?

 morning

....

Brothers, I do not consider that I have made it my
own. But one thing I do: forgetting what lies behind
and straining forward to what lies ahead . . .
Philippians 3:13 ESV

If we remain compelled by comfort, we're going to miss some of the greatest adventures that God has ever placed before man. In order to go anywhere, we've got to leave someplace. We must find a way to be driven by something that says I would leave every comfort behind to know the adventure of being compelled by nothing but the love of Christ. Does comfort or Christ drive your life?

☀ evening

Indeed, I count everything as loss because of the sur-
passing worth of knowing Christ Jesus my Lord. For
his sake I have suffered the loss of all things and count
them as rubbish, in order that I may gain Christ.
Philippians 3:8 ESV

Take a few minutes to think about the relationships in
your life such as the ones with your spouse, family and
friends. Do you operate in a mode of protection? If we
sign-up for a life compelled by comfort, we will live in a
rut of relational disasters if we are always trying to avoid
pain. This can also lead to a life of addiction. If we do not
have healthy relationships, we will turn to something
else. Life is filled with offers of happiness – if only we
have this, drive that, own this, wear that . . . it's an end-
less invitation. Yes, we all need comfort, but that comfort
must be found in God.

**Lord, I thank You for every blessing. I realize now
that some of those have come through the pain
and inconvenience in life. I desire Your presence
most of all.**

DAY 41

where is your focus?

 morning

For though we walk in the flesh, we are not waging war according to the flesh. For the weapons of our warfare are not of the flesh but have divine power to destroy strongholds. We destroy arguments and every lofty opinion raised against the knowledge of God, and take every thought captive to obey Christ . . .
2 Corinthians 10:3–5 ESV

Nothing will have a stronghold on you that has not been a focus in your life. This is true 100% of the time. A stronghold can only take its position when our mind is focused on it. It becomes a mental obsession; you think about it every day. The only way it's going to come down is if you keep your focus on the power of Christ and the divine weaponry He has given us to abolish it. Focus today on the power God has provided you to walk in freedom and peace.

☾ evening

For I feel a divine jealousy for you, since I betrothed you to one husband, to present you as a pure virgin to Christ. But I am afraid that as the serpent deceived Eve by his cunning, your thoughts will be led astray from a sincere and pure devotion to Christ.
2 Corinthians 11:2–3 ESV

There is nothing passive about the action of demolishing. Try and come up with a word that seems stronger than the word "demolish." It is a radical process and will take some focus. Every stronghold is a mental stronghold, but you have the power within you to break every single one. Rest in His power and provision knowing you are loved as you are, but equipped to pursue even more of His presence.

I commit my heart to You, Lord – my desires, pursuits and all that I can be in You. Thank You for the power You give me to demolish spiritual strongholds.

God still works in a BIG way!

 morning

He will be a joy and delight to you, and many will rejoice because of his birth . . . Luke 1:14

What happens when what comes naturally to others has to come supernaturally to you? The verse above is talking about the miracle of Jesus' birth, a joy and a delight. The word "joy" describes the emotion felt, but the word "delight" describes an action; it means to leap and dance and jump up and down for joy! **That's what takes place when you experience a miracle.** When something comes naturally for everybody else, but comes supernaturally for you there is necessary dancing, leaping and celebrating – and you wouldn't trade it for anything! Ask the Lord to work a miracle in your life and expect Him to come through in a BIG way!

evening

When it was time for Elizabeth to have her baby, she gave birth to a son. Her neighbors and relatives heard that the Lord had shown her great mercy, and they shared her joy. Luke 1:57–58

When we live to the glory of God, we show His goodness living through us. We live declaring what the Lord has done! We want others to know that miracles in our lives did not just happen by natural means. When we tell others, "The Lord my God has done this for me," I believe it is a thrill for Him. That is where we see the favor of God: in the delight of His response as we share this joy with everyone!

In spite of what the world believes, I serve a miracle -working God Who is fully active in my life.

a new thing is a good thing

 morning

See, I am doing a new thing! Now it springs up; do you not perceive it? I am making a way in the wilderness and streams in the wasteland. Isaiah 43:19

We need a fresh encounter with the Lord; the kind of thing that changes everything. When was the last time you had such an undeniable God encounter that, afterwards, your life could not possibly go back to normal? God moved in such a way that you had a brand-new normal. Let's prepare the way for the Lord. One of the traps that we fall into as Christians is that we figure out what we believe, and then we only read books that affirm what we already believed to be true. For some of us, we haven't had a genuine new idea come to us from the revelation of Scripture in ten solid years! We become all too comfortable in our current state.

⏺ evening

Brethren, I count not myself to have apprehended: but this one thing I do, forgetting those things which are behind, and reaching forth unto those things which are before, I press toward the mark for the prize of the high calling of God in Christ Jesus.
Philippians 3:13–14 KJV

Something I have learned from many, many years of ministry is that people are less likely to have a fresh encounter if they have had a long history with God than someone who is brand-new to God. The eyes of a new believer are astonished by the least little thing. Whether we are new believers or we've been seasoned in it for many years, we need a fresh encounter. We need to let God do a brand-new thing in us. We want to be part of an adventure, and God is all about taking us on the adventure of our lifetimes.

God, I don't want to settle for less than I can be in You. I open my heart to You once more to say, "Use me."

fully forgiven

 morning

Forgive us our debts, as we also have forgiven our debtors. Matthew 6:12

Do you believe you are fully forgiven? If we are going to forgive, there are a couple of things that we must understand. The first one is this: we must understand that forgiveness is for us. I want you to see that forgiveness is absolutely critical to our spiritual freedom. All of our sins, past, present and future, went to the cross of Christ with Him. They've all been nailed to the cross and He has dealt with every single one of them. You are fully forgiven so walk in that blessing today, and if you need to forgive someone, don't withhold it.

evening

And lead us not into temptation, but deliver us from the evil one. Matthew 6:13

Unforgiveness is an automatic stronghold. You never have to wonder if you have a stronghold, or area of captivity, if you have unforgiveness in your life. All it takes to qualify as a stronghold is that you become mentally hung up with it. There is nothing that has the capacity to lead us into greater temptation than unforgiveness. When we think we are unforgiven, or when we won't forgive, we are catapulted into a life of severe temptation, things like anger and entitlement. Choose to forgive, and don't give a foothold to the enemy.

Forgiven to live in freedom! Thank You, Jesus, for paying the price for my salvation and shedding Your blood for all my sins – past, present and future.

mercy, mercy, mercy!

 morning

Speak and act as those who are going to be judged by the law that gives freedom, because judgment without mercy will be shown to anyone who has not been merciful. Mercy triumphs over judgment.
James 2:12–13

God is all-wise, and we must realize that if we are not merciful people, we are going to have an encounter with God. We will have a season with God where we feel as though He is not pouring out favor in our misery. He is calling us to a place of mercy. Maybe you are going through a season where you have to make a choice between mercy or judgment. Mercy never means we do not speak truth. Mercy never means we act like we are blind. Mercy means you understand the current situation and you are choosing to have the heart of Christ toward the person in that state. We choose to see them beneath the surface and take into account that hurting people will hurt people. Mercy triumphs over judgment!

evening

The steadfast love of the LORD never ceases; his mercies never come to an end; they are new every morning; great is your faithfulness.
Lamentations 3:22–23 ESV

I don't always know if I'm going to be right or wrong in the way I deal with a situation, but if I am going to err on a side, let me err on the side of mercy. Let God say to me later, "You know what? You were a little overly merciful in that situation." Merciful does not mean gullible. I know very quickly in a situation whether I am working off of my own love or letting the love of Christ overtake my heart. Let Christ overtake your heart.

Lord, create in me a merciful heart that learns to speak the truth in love.

accepted just as I am

 morning

Blessed is he whose transgressions are forgiven, whose sins are covered. Blessed is the man whose sin the LORD does not count against him and in whose spirit is no deceit. Psalm 32:1–2 NIV 1984

I love the fact that we cannot fool God. I have tried to do it! I learned very early in life that when you come out of an abuse background, you tend to put up a front that you hope people will buy. You become a different person. Anytime we are living in that kind of masquerade, it will eventually fall down all around us. Spiritually we are called to live with integrity, and to be transparent, to be real. There is no need to put on a front for the One Who knows you best.

⭐●⭐ evening

Create in me a pure heart, O God, and renew a stead-fast spirit within me. Psalm 51:10

God can give us a pure heart even when we live an impure life. If you are like me, I tend to think that I am way past pure. I have learned and changed in great ways, but it is way too late for pure. Can you relate to me? The verse above does not say we have to have a pure life in our past. The verse says "pure in heart." Pure in heart can mean the very person that goes face down and says, "God, rescue me out of my depravity. I'm going to be honest with You Lord; I don't even know why I do what I do. I don't even know why. Rescue me." This is a pure heart. A pure life follows a pure heart.

It is a beautiful thing to be loved, accepted and forgiven by You, God. That is the spirit I want to show to those around me.

the Kingdom of God within you

 morning

. . . and he sent them out to proclaim the kingdom of God and to heal the sick. Luke 9:2

In this Kingdom mentality, healing and wholeness are always available. Christ says the secrets of the Kingdom are given to those who want to receive them. In other words, you are welcome to as much as you want to receive of the Kingdom. The Lord promises He will teach you and He will reveal it to you through His Word. However, if you do not want to hear it and you do not receive it, you are going to lose what you already had. I trust you will have a heart that continuously yearns for God to teach you. Proclaim the good news of the Kingdom today!

⋆ ● ⋆ evening

....

*"When you enter a town and are welcomed, eat what
is set before you. Heal the sick who are there and tell
them, 'The kingdom of God is near you.'"*
Luke 10:8–9 NIV 1984

There is complete wholeness when we see Jesus face-
to-face and His Kingdom comes. When we continuously
pray, *"thy kingdom come thy will be done on earth as it is
in heaven,"* the fullness of the Kingdom comes – and it is
apparent and obvious in all its bright array and glory. We
want to have eyes that do not just see, but also perceive,
and we want to have ears that not only hear; they truly
listen. The Kingdom of God in you presents wholeness
and healing to a broken world.

**Father, give me a heart for the Kingdom and use
me to bring healing and wholeness to a hurting
world. Let me have Your eyes, Father, to see people
as they are.**

God is at work in your story

 morning

....

And we know that for those who love God all things work together for good, for those who are called according to his purpose. Romans 8:28 ESV

God gives us a soft and tender heart toward Him instead of a heart that is calloused and hard. God causes us to see meaning in what we are going through, and helps us to see where He is working. But we have to truly open our hearts, our minds and eyes to receive. God is saying, "If you'll give your heart to me, I'll bring you a measure of understanding where a couple of puzzle pieces start coming together." You can't always see it at first, but God has a purpose in *all* that you have gone through.

☀ evening

....

For now we see in a mirror dimly, but then face to face. Now I know in part; then I shall know fully, even as I have been fully known. 1 Corinthians 13:12 ESV

I know there are many others like me who have a background of being abused, who wonder why. God is not the author of any kind of abuse or bondage or sin, but He did allow it. And why did He allow it? Because of what I was called to do and what you may be called to do. Every bit of what has come out of our brokenness has use in the Kingdom. When we begin to see that He can use it to bring ministry to others and bring compassion and humility to us as we serve people, it changes your outlook and gives you hope. It also brings healing!

I don't always understand my trials and tribulations, my pain and hurt, but I put my trust in You, God. I believe You can take everything in my life and redeem it for Your glory if I give it to You.

pain and purpose

 morning

....

I cry out to God Most High, to God who fulfills his purpose for me. Psalm 57:2 ESV

No matter what the Lord has allowed to cross your path, cry out to Him because somehow He is fulfilling your purpose. It will have some kind of impact on what you do here on this planet. If it has gone through the sifting of His hand, His good and faithful hand, and He allows it after you have asked to be delivered from it, somehow it has a place in the fulfillment of His purpose for you. **Remember this: you can live with pain more than you can live with purposelessness.** What you and I were born for, and what we long for, is to know that there is some reason we are on this planet; that the Creator of the entire universe chose us for this time and for this purpose.

☽ evening

....

*Blessed are the meek, for they shall inherit the earth.
Blessed are those who hunger and thirst for righteousness, for they shall be satisfied. Blessed are the merciful, for they shall receive mercy.* Matthew 5:5–7 ESV

I want to say this again – no matter what you are going
through, cry out to God, our Most High God who fulfills
His purpose for you. You are blessed and you have to
know it and believe it. You are blessed if you know you
need Him, because that's when we live face-to-face with
Him. You are blessed and will continue in the blessings
of God as you lay your life down for His purposes in you.

**I serve a God Who knows me by name, Who is a
good Father and loves to bless His children. I lay
down tonight thanking Him for His blessings.**

a reminder and a reason to seek Him first

morning

But he said, "I must preach the good news of the king-dom of God to the other towns also, because that is why I was sent." Luke 4:43 NIV 1984

I love that Jesus himself says, "I was sent to preach the gospel." And ultimately, Jesus is raising up disciples to be Kingdom-minded. When we think about our life priorities and the things that are important to us, God's Kingdom purposes must be on top of that list. Jesus goes on to give a wonderful promise saying, "Listen, if you will give yourself to one thing, My Kingdom, I will cause everything else of eternal value to come to you." What a promise! What a blessing!

evening

But seek first the kingdom of God and his righteous-
ness, and all these things will be added to you.
Matthew 6:33 ESV

He sees the plan from beginning to end, from eternity
to eternity. He sees the entire Kingdom agenda, and He
has placed us in a generation where our gifts will impact
others. In all of eternity, you were born in a time and place,
with gifts and talents that would work in tandem with the
body of believers on our planet at that time. We have a
Kingdom purpose in God's great plan and we must be
Kingdom-thinkers to find it. Is there something God is
calling you to do that you have been pondering in your
heart? I encourage you to take another step toward it.

Lord, help me to keep Your Kingdom purpose before
me. I *will* seek You first, for I believe Your promise
of "adding all these things unto you."

don't give
pride a ride

 morning

Likewise, you who are younger, be subject to the elders. Clothe yourselves, all of you, with humility toward one another, for "God opposes the proud but gives grace to the humble." 1 Peter 5:5 ESV

Do you ever quarrel with someone? Do you know why you quarrel? So much of our quarreling comes from our own pride, our own lack of humility. I want to tell you something: When we are full of pride, we are no longer just fighting against evil principalities or flesh and blood, we are now fighting with God. 1 Peter 5:5 tells us the reason we are fighting with God when we are full of pride. God opposes the proud, but gives grace to the humble. When we are puffed up with pride and when we are arrogant in our conflicts or any other kind of relational dimension, God is no longer fighting for us; He is fighting against us because He opposes pride. God fights for the humble. Do you find yourself walking in humility when you face conflict?

◉ evening

Love one another with brotherly affection. Outdo one another in showing honor. Romans 12:10 ESV

I want to ask you a question today. Just think it through and pray it through, and understand I'm never going to say anything that God hasn't already said and taught to me. Here is what I want to ask you today: so what if you do not win in other's eyes? If you know that you have the approval of God, you win. It is not the one who is the muddiest that wins the fight – it is the one with the least mud. How much mud are you wearing?

I pray for a peaceable spirit and the ability to get along with others and not push to always "win." Peace, joy and love are the characteristics I want to be known for in this world that's often filled with harsh words and conflict.

the joy of Jesus in you!

 morning

So that Christ may dwell in your hearts through faith
– that you, being rooted and grounded in love, may
have strength to comprehend with all the saints what
is the breadth and length and height and depth, and to
know the love of Christ that surpasses knowledge, that
you may be filled with all the fullness of God.
Ephesians 3:17–19 ESV

I love the righteousness, peace and joy that come with the power of the Kingdom that is within us. Not long ago, God gave me a picture of what our joy is like as believers. Our joy in the Holy Spirit is what makes us so contagious and magnetic to the people around us. Our joy in Christ is treasure to us. When we focus our eyes on the face of God and the way He speaks His promises over us, we cannot help but smile back. The world reacts to this kind of joy. They want whatever it is! Joy in the Holy Spirit! Share joy and God's love today to those around you.

☀ evening

Do not be afraid, little flock, for your Father has been pleased to give you the kingdom. Luke 12:32

Can you come to that realization today – that His Kingdom and His power live within you, within us all? We cannot necessarily see it sitting on our heads when we are staring in the mirror, but we are marked "Holy to the Lord." It is obvious who belongs to Him, and this Kingdom has been conferred to us as believers. The message here is to not be afraid, don't shrink back from what God wants to do in your life. You are precious to Him and valuable in the Kingdom.

The joy of the Lord is my strength and He is my rock in life. I'm glad to be counted on the Lord's side, and grateful He's on mine.

united we stand

 morning

For we do not wrestle against flesh and blood, but against the rulers, against the authorities, against the cosmic powers over this present darkness, against the spiritual forces of evil in the heavenly places.
Ephesians 6:12 ESV

The enemy has his own agenda. He has a counterfeit for anything God is doing. The very thing that got Satan kicked out of the presence of God was that he wanted to be the most high over his own kingdom. Therefore, he attacks God's people. One of the strongest truths of the Kingdom is that united we stand and divided we fall. In isolation, problems can become so pervasive and over-whelming but, when other Kingdom people come beside us, reminding us of the power that has been conferred upon us through the Kingdom, our mindset and circum-stances change! Who is God calling you to stand with?

☾ evening

....

Behold, how good and pleasant it is when brothers dwell in unity! Psalm 133:1 ESV

The Holy Spirit is what binds us together. Unity in the body is what the enemy will attack to try and divide us. We must begin to see where the enemy is coming against us. If he can divide the body, he can win battle after battle. All he has to do is get us to disagree over something that is usually secondary to the point. We have to unite. This is an all-out war we're in, a spiritual war, and it takes the body coming together as one people just the way Christ prayed.

I pray for the body of Christ to be one, just as Jesus prayed. Lord, help me to walk in unity with all my brothers and sisters in Christ, no matter what their background. We are family.

DAY 54

I will give You all the glory

 morning

....

The horse is made ready for the day of battle, but the victory belongs to the LORD. Proverbs 21:31 ESV

God has us figured out completely. Even when we truly believe our motive is pure, we sometimes think *we* are the reason for the victory – our talent, our personality, our spiritual gift at work. But one of the most important things to God is our humility. One of the most significant things you have to offer Him is your pure need for Him; the knowledge that you can accomplish nothing without His hand. All the lives you may touch, the changes for good you may see, are all to His glory! We just got to be part of the process. The victory belongs to the Lord, and it's a humbling privilege to be used in His purposes.

☾ evening

I am the LORD; that is my name; my glory I give to no other, nor my praise to carved idols. Isaiah 42:8 ESV

God knows how much success we can handle. He knows when we need to be humbled and reminded of our need for Him. When you walk with Jesus, defeat can turn into victory. You did not lose God, there simply needs to be times when we face up to our own self-centeredness. When we do, the victory comes.

You are God and I am not. I put my life in Your capable hands and realize for every victory and blessing I receive – You are behind them all!

DAY 55

humbled or exalted
. . . it's your choice

 morning

"For everyone who exalts himself will be humbled, and he who humbles himself will be exalted."
Luke 14:11 ESV

We are never going to win a battle we refuse to fight. Our true successes will always be in tandem with other people. We have a natural tendency in our great need for significance to be the "one." We want to be the hero. But God wants to bring victory to a people who recognize Who really brought it. If we are going to have a great story, it will display the exploits of many. God will give us opportunities to be the strong person in the group and then He will give us the opportunity to be the one who is suddenly weak. We always want to be the leader, but He does not let us get away with that. Suddenly we are the one in great need. Humility at its best! Regardless of how it looks, this is God's faithfulness to us!

⁎●⁎ evening

....

If one member suffers, all suffer together; if one member is honored, all rejoice together.
1 Corinthians 12:26 ESV

When you were at your lowest point, someone else came along and had the strength to help you up. When we pull out our swords for one another, big things happen. All through the heavens, they can hear the sound of swords slicing through the air as we stand up with one another and say, "I'm willing to go to battle with you. I will stand right beside you, and if this sword freezes to my hand, I will continue to attack in the name of our God with the Word of God." This is the beauty of the body of Christ.

Father, I thank You for those You've sent my way to help me in the battle. Use me to help others, and keep my heart humbled to receive help, too.

made whole and new in Christ

 morning

....

Therefore, if anyone is in Christ, he is a new creation.
The old has passed away; behold, the new has come.
2 Corinthians 5:17 ESV

In Christ, you have the right to be a whole person. Every single one of us has the right in Christ to be a whole and healthy individual. To have a healthy heart and mind is your right in Christ. When we begin to realize that we have some deep issues, that is the moment the enemy begins taunting us. He convinces us that if we ever did open that can of worms, we would not be able to cope. The enemy acts on his threats, and we must stand up to him – not in our own power – but with the Word. Claim who the Word says you are, "a new creation in Christ," with the old things passing away, dealt with and remembered no more by your Father.

evening

....

He drew me up from the pit of destruction, out of the miry bog, and set my feet upon a rock, making my steps secure. Psalm 40:2 ESV

The enemy knows when you come out on the other side of your past and present pains, you will rest in the health and healing of Jesus Christ. Your Deliverer will set your feet in a place of effectiveness, ministry and anointing, and the enemy is scared to death of this happening. *He has everything to lose in you getting healthy in Christ!* Whatever tricks he has to play to keep you from dealing with your issues, he's willing to use them. Today, claim your health and healing in Christ. It's your right as His child.

I am a new creation in Christ, and as I walk in newness of life, every step is secure because God is for me and the Holy Spirit is with me.

cast off!

 morning

Cast your burden on the LORD, and he will sustain you; he will never permit the righteous to be moved.
Psalm 55:22

When I was growing up, I really did have a heart for God. I also had an extremely self-destructive and very unhealthy mindset. I just kept cycling from one pit to the next. I came to a place where I began to really wake up to a deep desire to walk with God. In my mind, good Christians just pick themselves up and they walk on. I had no thought to possibly *open up my heart and let God heal me*. But, God knows every burden you carry and all the pain that has touched your life. God wants to wipe away your past and lift your burdens. Will you let Him?

☽ evening

....

Out of my distress I called on the Lord; the Lord an-swered me and set me free. Psalm 118:5 ESV

After truly dealing with my issues, I can tell you that in the process I became convinced that if I really dealt with them I was going to lose my mind! When the truth was that I was about to be set free. I was about to be healed and made whole! Christ gave me a renewed mind that does not conform even to our own world, or my past, but is transformed by Christ Himself. You have the right to claim your soundness of mind. Call on the Lord and claim it!

You are a faithful God Who hears my distress. I'm so grateful that You care and You act on my behalf to put me on a right path and set me free!

DAY 58

Lover of your soul

 morning

. . . for God gave us a spirit not of fear but of power and love and self-control. 2 Timothy 1:7 ESV

I'm not sure anything makes a bigger fool of us than a spirit of rejection. So often, our most foolish moments occur when we have been rejected. When we have been betrayed or rejected, we end up standing at a very important crossroad. We can choose to remain rejected, or we can choose to know that we have the spirit of Christ in us! And Christ has not given us a spirit of fear, but of power, of love and of a sound mind. When we end up in a situation where we have been rejected, remember the all-encompassing love of the Savior and the unchanging, unshakable fact that you are accepted in Christ, never rejected by Him.

evening

And he will be the stability of your times, abundance of salvation, wisdom, and knowledge; the fear of the Lord is Zion's treasure. Isaiah 33:6 ESV

Life will rock and roll you. It is a constant roller coaster. You wake up every morning with no idea what will happen that day, but God knows. Your God has not given you a spirit of fear, but one of power, of love and a sound mind. And He, your God, is your constant source of stability. Jesus is the Lover of your soul and Jesus is the Healer of your mind.

Look at all I have in Christ! I am blessed beyond measure. I want to keep my eyes on God's provision and purpose for me and not on the standards of this world; it's not my home anyway.

called to be in community

 morning

....

For nothing is hidden except to be made manifest;
nor is anything secret except to come to light.
Mark 4:22 ESV

It is so vital that we live in a community, as a part of the
body of Christ. We must know one another. You and I
need healthy people close enough to us that they have
enough courage to hold us accountable. We should
welcome them to do so. We must come to the point
where we can bring to light our struggles with each other.
Secrecy holds a tight grip on our minds. There is so much
secrecy in Christianity *because we do not want anyone*
to know we have issues in our lives. We are afraid others
have not been through the same things, yet most people
have. If you are not living in a community, ask the Lord
to place you in one.

evening

....

Not neglecting to meet together, as is the habit of some, but encouraging one another, and all the more as you see the Day drawing near. Hebrews 10:25 ESV

When we are living in isolation (and so much of the world is today), we can begin to think that a very dysfunctional situation is completely normal. When we are only operating within unhealthy walls, we start accepting it as God's will for our lives. It is not until we break free and live in a community that we realize we are living with something we ought *not* to be living with. We need to live in the light, and Jesus is light!

My community begins with the Father, Son and Holy Spirit, but it doesn't end there. I'm part of the family of God and that means having relationships.

says who?

 morning

There is therefore now no condemnation for those who are in Christ Jesus. Romans 8:1 ESV

You must go to God's Word to know what is true about yourself. Some of us have been conditioned our entire lives to think that we are stupid, that we are foolish, and that we will never be anything different than we are to-day. The enemy will try to convince us that everything behind us is a forecast of everything in front of us, and that is a lie! We have to know what God's Word says about us and cast down all negatives that have been put on us. Who does Jesus say you are? Believe it because *that* is the truth about you.

◦●◦ evening

In him we have obtained an inheritance, having been predestined according to the purpose of him who works all things according to the counsel of his will . . .
Ephesians 1:11 ESV

One of the things I want you to understand is that we can go through a season, it could be a couple of days, several months, or a few years, and it can catapult us into a time of unsound thinking. God's Word must be in the deepest recesses of our mind; even when we sleep we think differently, we dream differently and we meditate differently. That is how you get to know Jesus as you live off of Him day in and day out. When you experience victory in a place where you have had so many defeats, He is so proud of you.

Thank You, Lord, for the inheritance I have in You. You know my days and have things in store for me I cannot see . . . but I trust in You.

what are you thinking?

morning

Do not be conformed to this world, but be transformed by the renewal of your mind, that by testing you may discern what is the will of God, what is good and acceptable and perfect. Romans 12:2 ESV

Everything we do that has eternal value is going to grow out of our thought life. We all have strongholds, thoughts that lead us toward *carnality* or *timidity*. Both of these will keep us from being effective in what God has called us to do. Proverbs 23:7 (NKJV) says, *"For as a man thinks in his heart, so is he."* We're going to act out of *how* and *what* we think. If we are constantly obsessing over what is bothering us, then we will get in a cycle of defeated thoughts, which is a miserable place to be. We must replace our old thoughts with the new thoughts of Christ and what the Word says is true about us. Then we must believe it and act on it. Today is a fresh day to believe you are who God says you are!

⦁ evening

And whatever you do, in word or deed, do everything in the name of the Lord Jesus, giving thanks to God the Father through him. Colossians 3:17 ESV

What you choose to do, what you do on purpose, is framed by your thought life. That is where fertile ground is and that is where the change takes place. Our thoughts are the starting place – we make a decision to begin to *act* differently. But remember, most of the time it doesn't happen overnight; it is a process. We will never do it simply based on our own determination; it's got to be a change of mind along with a change of heart. Renew your mind with the Word of God and let those thoughts shape your mind, which then shapes your desires and, ultimately, your actions.

Lord, help me think on this: " *. . . whatever is true, whatever is honorable, whatever is just, whatever is pure, whatever is lovely, whatever is commendable, if there is any excellence, if there is anything worthy of praise, think about these things.*" (Philippians 4:8 ESV)

every stronghold can be brought down

 morning

"... *and you will know the truth, and the truth will set you free.*" John 8:32 ESV

In my personal strongholds – my areas of bondage and addiction – I had to go through my own process of breaking free in my relationship with God. Once I truly addressed them, they lost their power over me. Think about this: you are in the middle of a decision and you can feel yourself moving in the wrong direction. What is happening in that moment before you do that habitually destructive thing? For me, it was insecurity. For some reason, something would well up inside of me and I would feel insecure, full of self-doubt and self-loathing and ... boom! I made the wrong decision once again. It took me years to realize God and I have seen so many things lose their power over me, but I hadn't addressed the insecurity by itself and focused on that one thing. Let God speak to you through His Word and tell you what His thoughts are about any strongholds in your life. His Word in your heart and His grace over your life will subdue that which has defeated you.

☀ evening

But he said to me, "My grace is sufficient for you, for my power is made perfect in weakness." Therefore I will boast all the more gladly about my weaknesses, so that the power of Christ may rest upon me.
2 Corinthians 12:9 ESV

We are in a spiritual battle every day. You can have sincere, pure devotion to Christ, and the enemy will still attempt to seduce your mind. Every single stronghold is a mental stronghold. It is very important that we become aware of our strongholds. We have to be able to name them. We have to be able to claim God's Word on them. Take some time to ask the Lord what could be holding you back from His purposes in your life. Rest in the power of His might because you are not fighting in your own strength, *"Not by might, nor by power, but by my Spirit, says the LORD of hosts"* (Zechariah 4:6 ESV). It is a good thing to be on the Lord's side in life!

Lord, I thank You that in the battle You are with me. In my weakness, You are strong, and in my victories, You are glorified.

the Word in you can be a word for others

 morning

It is written: "I believed; therefore I have spoken." With that same spirit of faith we also believe and therefore speak . . . 2 Corinthians 4:13 NIV 1984

When you and I allow God to put to death something destructive in our own lives, it brings somebody else who is near us to life. This is a most marvelous concept! Again today, believe the Word from the Lord and pray that Word. Receive that Word then speak that Word. Maybe in the course of the day, you will get a chance to share that Word with someone that needs to hear it. Dying to self is not only about us, it opens doors, we may never have seen, to speak life to others. May your heart be full of His Word today and your spirit open to His leading. There is adventure out there!

☀ evening

I will walk about in freedom, for I have sought out your precepts. Psalm 119:45

Scripture never gets tired. It is alive and active all the time. For instance, when I was trying to walk in victory over the addiction that I had, I looked up fifteen scriptures that really spoke to my situation. I personalized them in prayer with my own name, and I would pray those things every single day. When I began to realize I was not thinking so much about what they were saying, I would go to a new set; I would write down some more. This way I did not grow tired because I was putting my burden on the Word of God instead of on myself. When we truly believe God's Word, we seek it out. We think on it and it becomes a part of our life. There simply is no substitute for the life-changing Word of God.

Give me a desire to read Your Word and believe every promise beginning with the beauty of grace. Help me to receive that, Lord.

the tale of the tongue

 morning

Death and life are in the power of the tongue, and those who love it will eat its fruits. Proverbs 18:21 ESV

When we are immersed in God's Word, we are living and breathing victory. It is marvelous and miraculous! We do not give enough credit to the power of our tongue. The most powerful built-in instrument we have – whether you are saved, lost, know Christ, or don't know Christ – is your mouth. God's words are omnipotent; He speaks, it happens. Therefore, since His words are omnipotent, our words are potent. We use our mouths for such opposing purposes that we have no power when it comes time to use it in the spirit. Whether it is gossip, or whether it is profanity, it is exactly what the book of James talks about when it says you are using your mouth to bless and curse. And it says, this ought not to be. We want our tongues to be used as instruments of supernatural power. If you feel as though you lack power in the supernatural, maybe the Lord is waiting on you to surrender your tongue to Him.

evening

"Woe to me!" I cried. "I am ruined! For I am a man of unclean lips, and I live among a people of unclean lips, and my eyes have seen the King, the LORD Almighty." Isaiah 6:5

The prophet Isaiah's heart was to think purely, and to speak purely and godly before the world. In this passage, he is asking God to cleanse his heart and his lips. He speaks of "taking coals off the altar," spiritually speaking, and touching them to our lips to cleanse our mouths. We are a people of unclean lips and we live around a people of unclean lips! But, when our tongues are sanctified and we start breathing in the Word and start speaking that Word, we will experience His power. We have the ultimate, wireless connection to God. It is always secure . . . no dropped calls! Look at the promise God makes in the closing prayer tonight.

Call to me and I will answer you, and will tell you great and hidden things that you have not known (Jeremiah 33:3 ESV). I *will* call Lord, and then I will *listen* for Your voice.

God is FOR you!

 morning

What then shall we say to these things? If God is for us, who can be against us? Romans 8:31 ESV

Make sure that your battle is with the enemy and not with God. This is a very, very important principle and I want to repeat it: God is *always* for us and *never* against us. And although He is always for us, when we are in pride, sometimes the best way He can show He is for us is to work in opposition to us. Then we will understand He is not leading us the way we are trying to go. In those times, the enemy will work on you to try and get you to think, "God is against me!" But, today, I'm encouraging you to begin by thanking the Lord for being faithful and FOR you!

·*●·* evening

···

"God resists the proud, but gives grace to the humble."
1 Peter 5:5 NKJV

God is for us, but when we're all puffed up in our own flesh, He has concerns. If you want to beat back pride, you need to learn to go face down before God. It's only when we go to our knees in humility that we can really see if it's the enemy working against us, or God getting on our case because of pride. Make sure the one we're fighting is not God, because we cannot fight a battle with God and win. I'm just going to tell you that up front. It's rigged! It really is!

I choose this day to once again declare that I'm on Your side. I want all You have for me, God. I remind myself again that You are the Potter and I am the clay.

what is "it" for you?

 morning

Set your minds on things that are above, not on things that are on earth. Colossians 3:2 ESV

Have you ever gotten what you thought you wanted and were still unhappy? The reason for this is we become convinced that one thing would be "it" for us and we have set ourselves up to be emotional vacuums. It happens over and over again. We try to make our fleshly desires our "everything," but it will never work. Growing into wholeness emotionally is coming to the realization that those things will not cut it; they will never fully satisfy. We have got to have Jesus. We will have things we want, but He alone has to be our ultimate fulfillment and pursuit in life.

☽ evening

Trust in him at all times, O people; pour out your heart before him; God is a refuge for us. Psalm 62:8 ESV

If you begin to realize that you are under oppression to your own emotions, there comes a time when you must simply get up. When you put pressure on your closest loved ones to try and help you become emotionally satisfied, something must change. You cannot keep doing the same thing the same way and expect something different to happen. It is time to do something different! I'm not saying with someone different, especially when it comes to families. God longs for us to pour every single one of those emotions, no matter how toxic, out right before Him freely. Next time we're tempted to pour into ourselves or someone else who will listen "one more time," consider what it is that we need to pour out to Him.

Jesus, I'm reminded that You alone know all of me, and still accept me for who I am. Help me to be real with You and not avoid You. Like Simon Peter said to You, "*Lord, to whom shall we go? You have the words of eternal life . . .*" (John 6:68 ESV).

His words are life to you!

 morning

So shall my word be that goes out from my mouth; it shall not return to me empty, but it shall accomplish that which I purpose, and shall succeed in the thing for which I sent it. Isaiah 55:11 ESV

The Bible is a whole book of powerful, life-giving words. Jesus told us His words are life and spirit to us. Yet for most of my young life, they just stayed on the page and away from the reality of my own soul until I chose to believe them. That is the only way it gets in and empowers us from the inside out. Do you believe God's Word? Nothing is so big that it cannot be demolished by the divine power of weaponry you put in your hands through Christ Jesus. Read today's scripture again, putting your name anywhere you want in it, even more than once. That personalizes it and sounds like God is talking to you! He is!

☾ evening

....

For our struggle is not against flesh and blood, but against the rulers, against the authorities, against the powers of this dark world and against the spiritual forces of evil in the heavenly realms.
Ephesians 6:12 NIV

"Struggle" in the Greek language does not mean army-to-army, it means person-to-person. It's when you're going at it in "hand-to-hand" combat against an enemy right in front of you. In your walk of faith, many people can help you in your battle, but nobody can fight it for you. Victory comes when you allow God to empower you. He is not looking to just make you a victor. He is most interested in relationship, looking for a heart that desires to be immersed in His Spirit!

Lord, there is none like You. Thank You for allowing me to walk with You, talk with You and hear Your heart's desires for me. I fight the good fight of faith, but never without You!

wonderfully made and precious in His sight

 morning

* * *

Because you are precious in my eyes, and honored, and I love you, I give men in return for you, peoples in exchange for your life. Isaiah 43:4 ESV

One of the things I long to see God accomplish in each of our lives is the astounding, and sudden, realization that you are precious to Him. We can feel like we are in such a large crowd that we tend to think, "He really wasn't saying that to me." We will let someone else receive a word from God, but not allow ourselves. Please stop thinking that all of the profound works God wants to do are going to be in your church leaders and people that you view as particularly gifted. You are gifted too! The first 13 words of that scripture (yes, go count them) need to be memorized. They are true for you today and every day, so carry them in your heart and don't let go.

evening

I will give thanks to the LORD with my whole heart; I will recount all of your wonderful deeds.
Psalm 9:1 ESV

The enemy wants us to believe we hardly deserve to be forgiven, and certainly do not deserve to be used. This could not be further from God's truth. So often, we don't believe what He did for us. We fool ourselves into believing God sees humility in us, when we don't even see ourselves as forgiven. God calls that unbelief. When the enemy tempts us with self-condemnation, instead of going there with him, we must go to our Savior, Who has already delivered us, and once again give Him praise! Once the enemy realizes that your new reaction is going to be praise, he will not do it long. If there is one thing the enemy does not want to provoke you to do, it is to praise and show gratitude to God.

I will give thanks to the Lord God for I have been created in Him, and reborn by the precious blood of Jesus. I am forgiven, gifted and have a purpose in God's plan for this fallen world.

the freedom of forgiveness

 morning

If we confess our sins, he is faithful and just to forgive us our sins and to cleanse us from all unrighteousness. 1 John 1:9 ESV

Be real before God. If we are, we will know the power of His healing. What is it that is stopping us from getting up and moving on? The enemy will use guilt and condemnation to keep us stuck in the same place, and we feel like we can't even go to church and hold our heads up because we remember what happened in our past. Sometimes we do not even know what it is; we are just stuck. Sometimes we're paralyzed by unforgiveness toward ourselves. Does something have you paralyzed, or a loved one, or someone God has brought in your life? There is one very important word in that scripture about forgiveness. It's the small word, "all." That covers it. Believe it.

evening

And he said to him, "I will come and heal him."
Matthew 8:7 ESV

In the midst of my own struggles, it took years before I was experiencing full freedom. I went through layers and layers of bondage. It was a deep stronghold, and it took some long and radical work. But, in the process, by the time my healing came, I knew my Healer a whole lot better than I knew my healing, and I was in love forever!

I serve a healing Jesus Who can touch body, soul and spirit. Thank You for forgiveness and a new life, and for the ongoing work of healing all my hurts if I will only give them to You.

the one and only you!

 morning

Peter turned and saw the disciple whom Jesus loved following them, the one who also had leaned back against him during the supper and had said, "Lord, who is it that is going to betray you?" John 21:20 ESV

I find it a little amusing that John describes himself as, "The disciple whom Jesus loved." If you are not careful, this one will kill your spiritual zeal: comparison. There are many ways that we compare ourselves with others in the body of Christ. The thing is we are all in a race, and the enemy loves for us to get our eyes off Jesus and on our efforts, talents and calling in comparison to others. That's why I think it's important to change our concept from a race to a chase. We are not racing one another! We are on the same team and our goal is to finish what He has called <u>us</u> to do.

evening

I praise you, for I am fearfully and wonderfully made.
Wonderful are your works; my soul knows it very well.
Psalm 139:14 ESV

Comparison will be the death of us. It will completely steal our joy and it will definitely undermine our giftedness. If we think we are called to do the same thing as someone else, we almost lose it. This is the incredible thing about Jesus. He designed us so uniquely that we could never be someone's exact duplicate. It is in our DNA to be completely unique and set apart. As life progresses, we become a product of bits and pieces of all the different mentors that God has used to sow into our lives. Take a moment to reflect on those who have been a blessing to you and give thanks. It's a beautiful thing to be just you!

In all the world there is only one of me. In the body of Christ I was created to be . . . uniquely qualified for "such a time as this." God, I once again give my life to this time and place where You brought me.

God cares about your hurts

morning

And falling to the ground he heard a voice saying to him, "Saul, Saul, why are you persecuting me?" And he said, "Who are you, Lord?" And he said, "I am Jesus, whom you are persecuting." Acts 9:4–5 ESV

It is of extreme importance to your healing and to the health of your soul that you know when anything happens to you, Christ takes it personally. He cares about His Church. It was His people that were being persecuted in this discourse from Acts, chapter 9. Paul is saying to the voice, "I don't know who you are. I don't even know what to do with you." The voice of Jesus replies, "You know what you do to them. Why are you persecuting me?" Paul says, "But, I'm persecuting *them*." To which he hears, "What you are doing to *them*, you do to me. What you do to touch the hair of their head, to trouble their lives, you have done personally to me." What I see in this scripture is God taking your hurt personally. I trust the reminder that your Lord and Savior cares so personally for you just made your day!

⭑●⭑ evening

....

Indeed, I count everything as loss because of the surpassing worth of knowing Christ Jesus my Lord. For his sake I have suffered the loss of all things and count them as rubbish, in order that I may gain Christ.
Philippians 3:8 ESV

All of us are drawn to give way to one life pursuit, one driving force, something that makes us feel alive; something that makes us feel zeal and passion. We are all after that one thing that we cannot get enough of, never conquer, that we can never completely figure out. All of us are after the one thing that could sweep us off of our feet and I am telling you once again, Jesus is the One! He is it: the ultimate, life-long chase.

Lord, I want to think I found You, but, really, You found me and captured my heart. I give You that heart tonight – all of it, all of my hurts as well as my hopes. And I will run after You for all my days.

live to forgive

 morning

No temptation has overtaken you that is not common to man. God is faithful, and he will not let you be tempted beyond your ability, but with the temptation he will also provide the way of escape, that you may be able to endure it. 1 Corinthians 10:13 ESV

I could have easily titled this one, "Forgive to live!" It is so easy to be an offended person and turn right around and be an offensive person! All those daily offenses you might suffer today on the part of others can be used to practice forgiveness. We must learn to forgive in the gravest, deepest, most hurtful wounds of our lives. We can feel all alone in our struggle to forgive, but we have been told in God's Word that *everything* we've gone through and will go through, our brothers and sisters throughout the world have also endured. The lie of the enemy is that you are the only one, and he tries to ramp up your anger from there. Don't let him.

evening

Each heart knows its own bitterness, and no one else can share its joy. Proverbs 14:10

I know the verse above can seem a little bit disturbing. This is one of those Bible verses that make you just sit back in your chair and ponder for a little while. It does not mean we do not share joy with one another; it is saying that in the extremities of the human experience, we will often find that there is a sense that no one "gets it" besides us. This is certainly true of bitterness. You can easily feel no one understands. But there is always One Who does.

Whether I am hurting, or on a "mountain-top" experience, You, Lord are with me. You are my constant Companion, the Healer of my heart, the One Who teaches me there is life after forgiveness and bitterness.

the Lord
your Healer

 morning

His pleasure is not in the strength of the horse, nor his delight in the legs of the warrior; the Lord delights in those who fear him, who put their hope in his unfailing love. Psalm 147:10–11

The Lord binds up the brokenhearted, and binding is a process. He doesn't just point to it and say, "Be healed." He can if He wants to; He can do that with our broken hearts, broken bodies and sickness of any kind. But in the area of broken-heartedness, it seems to always be the type of binding up that gives you a picture of a process, not an instant healing! He wants us to fall in love with Him as our Healer. He wants us to really know Him through it, where we come out of it more in love with Him than anything we could possibly see or touch.

☀ evening

The Lord builds up Jerusalem; he gathers the exiles of Israel. He heals the brokenhearted and binds up their wounds. Psalm 147:2–3

The whole chapter of Psalm 147 is about exile; a people that rebelled themselves into distance from God. The exiles had caused their own broken-heartedness. They wounded themselves with their exile, so therefore they think they ought not get any healing for it, it is their own fault. Have you self inflicted? He can heal you just as easily from what someone has done to you as what you have done to yourself and vice versa. We serve a God Who restores, heals, comforts and most importantly, is a God of grace.

As I quiet my heart before You, Lord come with healing words of love and correction. I submit my heart fully to You. I know You can heal every hurt and restore me to fullness of joy and a renewed sense of the purposes and plans You have for me.

united against the real enemy

 morning

"For where two or three are gathered in my name, there am I among them." Matthew 18:20 ESV

The enemy does not want us to share the message of restoration and reconciliation with those around us, especially regarding marriage. The truth is you have an enemy in common, an enemy out to destroy you. But there is something about uniting as a couple and realizing, "Our struggle is not with flesh and blood. It is not between us!" It's this unseen force of evil that comes to wreck all things that God has built up in your marriage and family, to bring it to absolute disintegration. Don't let the fight divide you, but rather, let it push you to stick together as a couple or family and become even stronger. Remember if two or three gather in His name, He is there!

☾ evening

....

*Every word of God proves true; he is a shield to those
who take refuge in him.* Proverbs 30:5 ESV

I think many times Christians focus too much on the sin
when they should be putting all their attention on Jesus.
All worship is, in its essence, focus. When we are in a
worship service, we are focusing on God, and we can
unintentionally do that with the enemy, too. We get so
obsessed with the reality of spiritual warfare that we end
up putting too much focus on Satan instead of resisting
what he is doing in us. The Word is your shield. Believers
who know the Word of God and what He is doing in the
heavens can walk steadfastly in this world.

**My thoughts are lifted toward You, Lord. When I
remember the work You are doing in me, my heart
is filled with thanksgiving, and my spirit is lifted
knowing that You are not finished with me yet.**

He created the "makeover!"

 morning

"Behold, I am the LORD, the God of all flesh. Is anything too hard for me?" Jeremiah 32:27 ESV

Even if you have gone through a divorce, or two, or three, or perhaps you have never married and have no desire to, you need to know that healthy, happy relationships are possible. There is a security that comes to us when we see a living example of a couple that has made it, or even when we see healthy lifelong friendships. They are rare! My parents lived to be married 54 years but they did not retain intimacy and closeness. They did not let themselves be restored back to a place to truly live in love. People must see what God can do to change lives so we can be rich in relationships. Every crisis doesn't have to lead to despair or death of some kind. God is in the business of reconciling! He is a Restorer!

☾ evening

Humble yourselves before the Lord, and he will exalt you. James 4:10 ESV

In marriage, and relationships in general, will we walk in humility or humiliation? God just wants us to bend our knee to Him and ask Him for help. In our anguish, He longs for us to cry out to Him. His desire is not to shame us publicly. Anything that becomes public between us and the Lord is because in the secret places we resisted His voice. Please know His goal is not our humiliation. He asked for us to have humility before Him. This character trait is a foundation for every other relationship we have in our lives, especially marriage.

God, You gave a great guideline for daily living to your prophet Micah and I pray it tonight: *He has showed you, O man, what is good. And what does the LORD require of you? To act justly and to love mercy and to walk humbly with your God* **(Micah 6:8 NIV 1984).**

I hear what you're saying!

 morning

Know this, my beloved brothers: let every person be quick to hear, slow to speak, slow to anger . . .
James 1:19 ESV

Sometimes in the middle of conflict it is best to simply say, "I hear you." We all want to be heard. You are not required to feel exactly the same way as another person, but you can at least hear them out. Don't let a present trouble steal all the joy you shared with that person in the past, or in the future. You must realize that in the midst of your disagreement with someone special to you, that you are on the same team. You are *for* each other, not *against* one another.

● evening

....

A soft answer turns away wrath, but a harsh word stirs up anger. Proverbs 15:1 ESV

In any close relationship, when people stop having any kind of conflict whatsoever, they've stopped having any kind of communication. When you care and feelings are involved in relationship, you will have conflict. When you are in a conversation and all of the sudden you can tell it brings some kind of offense, stop and clarify what you are trying to say. You can either stop right then and say it a different way, or you can just go on, escalate the argument and volume and put more friction between the two of you. Stop. Listen. And like your mother said, "Use your *inside* voice!"

I don't always have to win the argument, but I do need to communicate. Help me to say what's on my heart and hear what is on another's heart.

sometimes you just want to run away . . . and I say, "OK!"

morning

You are a hiding place for me; you preserve me from trouble; you surround me with shouts of deliverance.
Psalm 32:7 ESV

The enemy wants us to think it is the most selfish thing to say, "You know what, I'm checking out for a little while." We must learn to set the less important things aside to make time for the Lord Who sustains us. What some might call selfish is actually time made for the true ministry of the Holy Spirit. He's our Shelter and our Hiding Place. Psalm 32 is filled with encouraging words describing the grace, comfort and forgiveness we find in Christ. It's OK to break away and run to Jesus to find shelter when you can't get full. Take a break and just be with Jesus!

evening

He who dwells in the shelter of the Most High will abide in the shadow of the Almighty. Psalm 91:1 ESV

When life is moving along rapidly, be sure your spiritual tank is full and being ministered to by the Lord Jesus. You're awake in Him and you don't give way to random compulsions. However, as soon as we start moving from a full tank down toward empty, the emptier we get, the more compulsive we get. Those compulsions are attempts to fill the emptiness with something other than the Spirit of Christ. When I cannot get full, or I cannot do anything enough; eat enough, drink enough, cannot get enough activity or affirmation, I know I am running on empty! I encourage you to read Psalms 32 and be refreshed with the goodness of our God!

Lord, come and fill me anew as I keep my mind set on You.

keeping it real

 morning

. . . He is a double-minded man, unstable in all his ways. James 1:8 ESV

What we cultivate in secret will ultimately be lived out in our public lives. I know the pain and suffering of living a secret life and the misery of duplicity. What would happen if what we most cultivated in secret was intimacy with the Lord Jesus Christ? What if your public life with Christ was only exceeded by your private life with Christ? I've said this to the Lord over and over again, "Do not let me be more passionate about You in public than I am about You in private! I want my private relationship with You to be more passionate than anything I could ever show out in public! I want it to be real, I want it to be true, or I don't want it at all."

evening

This is the message we have heard from him and proclaim to you, that God is light, and in him is no darkness at all. 1 John 1:5 ESV

For a long time my duplicity was not an external manifestation, it was just in my heart and brain. I had changed my behaviors, but I had not changed the way I thought. I still thought in defeat. I began seeing that God wanted to cultivate in the depths of my heart, in the closets where I had the hidden things of my life. When Jesus walks into those dark, deep hidden places of our heart, they are brought to light!

Father, I ask for Your help to be real with You and enjoy the blessings of a life covered by grace.

there's a time to heal

 morning

. . . A time to kill, and a time to heal; a time to tear down, and a time to build up . . . Ecclesiastes 3:3

This may be for you, or for someone God brings to mind as you read. Is it your time to heal? We can do all of the Bible studies in the world, but if we do not apply them, if we just eat the seed and do not sow it into the reality of our lives, we're not going to be any different. I want to challenge you to give it 30 days; 30 days of intense healing. What if, every day for a month you said, "Lord, I'm seeking this healing in this one area"? Get someone to hold you accountable and also to pray for you. Tell them, "I want to humble myself before you. I've got a deep wound that has caused me to have deeply rooted hurt and resentment and I'm tired of it." Give it to God every moment of every day for 30 days. He will heal you!

☾ evening

....

The LORD builds up Jerusalem; he gathers the out-casts of Israel. He heals the brokenhearted and binds up their wounds. Psalm 147:2–3 ESV

This scripture is telling us that God binds up the wounded. In the area of broken-heartedness it seems to always be a "binding up," which gives you a picture of a process, and not just a quick healing! In this process, He wants us to fall in love with Him as Healer. I don't care how responsible you are for your own broken-heartedness. I don't care if you knew going into the relationship that it was going to be the death of you, and you did it anyway. I don't care if you sinned yourself into oblivion and dug your own pit. He's come to bind up your broken-heartedness even if it came at the hammer of our own hand. Stop letting your guilt block your healing. God is right there with healing and hope.

What a faithful and loving God You are. Thank You for being my Healer – body, soul and spirit – encouraging me to be whole in You and binding up every wound I reveal to You.

what is that one thing?

 morning

But seek first the kingdom of God and his righteous-ness, and all these things will be added to you.
Matthew 6:33 ESV

What could we find that we could chase for the rest of our lives and never get tired of it? There is one thing we will naturally chase after – our life passion. It's what we are chasing down with our time, our money and our energies. We lose our passion when we try to multitask and do way too many things at one time. There is only one thing in all the world you can make your life pursuit and your life priority, and everything else of value will be added to it.

◉ evening

So flee youthful passions and pursue righteousness, faith, love, and peace, along with those who call on the Lord from a pure heart. 2 Timothy 2:22 ESV

There will never be a single person that lives chasing Jesus Christ that will get to their death bed and say, "I really should have chosen something else." I don't know what God has ahead for you, but I know it is going to be something that doesn't come naturally to you; and it is not something attainable by your own talent or your own abilities. It will be beyond what you could do without Him. Whatever He has for you is something so dramatic, that it will be obvious it must be God because it could not possibly be you!

I will seek You, Lord, and Your ways. I know my life has eternal purpose and my place in Your plans will bring me peace.

loving God and loving others

 morning

....

And he answered, "You shall love the Lord your God with all your heart and with all your soul and with all your strength and with all your mind, and your neighbor as yourself." Luke 10:27 ESV

All of us have had people in our life that were hard to like, let alone love. But, we do not live in isolation, nor has God told us to. Sometimes when we are hurt we choose to pull away, withdrawing from everyone. However, you will only become colder and colder toward people until you take seriously the priority of God's command, which is to love the Lord our God with all our heart, soul, mind and strength and *love others* as we love ourselves. Love requires risk.

· ● · evening

Beloved, let us love one another, for love is from God, and whoever loves has been born of God and knows God. 1 John 4:7 ESV

You cannot love God without loving others. I want to do that at times, but it doesn't work that way. We are not just vessels for God's love to take in all we can and keep it for ourselves, there is to be an overflow of His love "splashing" out onto other people. In a world filled with heartache and sorrow, including your own, God comes to heal your heart so you can be a healing, loving source for someone in need. There *is* an overflow in you.

Father, I thank You for Your unfailing love to me. Help me to not hold back from loving others, but to let Your love flow through me.

matters of the heart

 morning

And the peace of God, which transcends all understanding, will guard your hearts and your minds in Christ Jesus. Philippians 4:7

Never doubt that your God cares about matters of the heart. When your heart is broken, life can change in a big way. Decisions can be made that take you down the right path or the wrong path. I want you to see today, paying close attention, that God esteems broken-heartedness. You can go through big problems, or a simple matter of great importance to you, and God will pursue you for healing. God wants to bring you complete healing. Can I say it like this? Your heart is a big deal to God!

☽ evening

But the Helper, the Holy Spirit, whom the Father will send in my name, he will teach you all things and bring to your remembrance all that I have said to you.
John 14:26 ESV

We are told in the gospel of John that the Holy Spirit will remind us of the things that Jesus has taught us. I love that concept. I've been sharing about how our hearts are broken in so many ways – some of them truly great and devastating losses such as deaths, hard breakups, a separation, divorce or a broken engagement. I want you to know if you've had your heart broken in any of those ways that you legitimately need the attentiveness of God. This is the time to ask the Holy Spirit to show you the areas of your heart that God wants to heal.

I will guard my heart as I renew my mind in the Word. Father, I'm thankful for Your healing and the help of the Holy Spirit when I go through rough times, hurts and disappointments.

God not only knows you, He "gets" you

  morning

O LORD, You have searched me and known me. You know my sitting down and my rising up; You understand my thought afar off. You comprehend my path and my lying down, And are acquainted with all my ways. Psalm 139:1–3 NKJV

This scripture is so unique because nothing surpasses this brief segment of scripture that describes so many attributes of the greatness and transcendence of our God. It talks about His omniscience – He knows everything. It talks about His omnipresence – He is everywhere. And it talks about His omnipotence – He is all powerful and can create from absolutely nothing. It talks about God being all in all. You owe it to yourself to read all of Psalm 139 and see how much our great God is concerned and aware of you – every bit of you. You are fully known, but even better, fully loved!

☀ evening

And he who searches our hearts knows the mind of the Spirit, because the spirit intercedes for the saints in accordance with God's will. Romans 8:27 NIV 1984

God literally searches your heart. He finds you interesting, intriguing, and He is continually seeing what He's developing in you before it even erupts into your behaviors or your speech. Our God continually searches us out. Isn't there something in us that wants to be pursued? Don't we desire someone to chase after us? There is something invigorating about knowing that the God of the universe in all His perfection, the valiant Warrior of the ages, seeks me out and searches for me.

I do not fear my God. He is a loving Father Who has been interested in me from the beginning of time. The One Who knows me best, loves me most!

open your heart
to hear Him

 morning

For this reason I kneel before the Father . . .
Ephesians 3:14

Have you ever just dropped to your knees in prayer? There are times when the Spirit of God is prodding us to kneel and humble ourselves before the Father, but we sometimes fight that feeling, that leading. When something says, "Go face-down!" why don't we just go face-down instead of finishing up our mascara? Think about it. You might not be able to do that in a service where you are among others, but what about at home? Do you have a "thank-you" dance in you? Go right ahead. Do you have a "kneel" in you? Go right ahead. It's just you and Jesus and those can be the best times of your life.

evening

....

And I pray that you, being rooted and established in love, may have power, together with all the saints, to grasp how wide and long and high and deep is the love of Christ. Ephesians 3:17–18 NIV 1984

Paul is talking here about the "power to grasp" the enormous truth of God's love. It's not something that just comes from reading the statement, it's not something that comes naturally to us; it is a supernatural unction. I love that word! "Unction" is an anointing, a divine power on us, that is working through us. What if, as a direct result of our reading today, we went to our work place, or into relationships, or responded to people around us and inside our homes with *a new power and revelation* of the depth and height and breadth of God's love for us? What if, supernaturally, that happened to you today? I want that, don't you?

Let me be real before You, Father, let me know the depths of Your love and let that understanding be revealed in my life as I share it with others.

guard your heart ... God lives there!

 morning

Keep your heart with all diligence, For out of it spring the issues of life. Proverbs 4:23 NKJV

If we want to know what it means to guard our hearts, we need to see God in action guarding His heart. God is constantly maintaining His love. He guards Himself against diminishing love. We guard our hearts *from* people; God guards His heart *for* people. No matter what you've experienced, He will not diminish in His love for you. When we go through a time where we have reaped what we have sown, when we bear some consequences of our own actions, God has frozen His love for us. He never sets His abounding love for you aside. The biggest priority we have is not what we are protecting our hearts against, but what we are protecting our hearts for. He guarded His heart consistently so that it would overflow constantly with an abounding kind of love. Is that the way we guard?

☀ evening

....

The Spirit Himself bears witness with our spirit that we are children of God, and if children, then heirs – heirs of God and joint heirs with Christ . . .
Romans 8:16–17 NKJV

If you are in Jesus Christ, you are housing the very Spirit of Christ. Let that sense of value skyrocket within you. When you feel insignificant and insecure, do you think you don't have value? You're walking around with the very Spirit of Christ in you. Every step you take, every place you go, every relationship you engage in, He never leaves you nor forsakes you. That is a sense of significance.

Lord, help me to guard my heart so Your love can be released *in* me, *through* me and be the blessing to others like me who need to know they are loved.

keep your confidence in Him

 morning

Let us then approach God's throne of grace with confidence, so that we may receive mercy and find grace to help us in our time of need. Hebrews 4:16

Your confidence in Christ is your right. Maybe something happened to cause you to lose your confidence – something at work, something in your serving life or your relational life that you really put effort into. These are times that can give us a huge hit in the area of our confidence. But when you receive the Lord Jesus Christ, His very Spirit takes residency in us. His competence and His confidence come to dwell inside of us. However, if we receive Christ as our Savior, but never recognize and by faith believe Him to be our Healer and Restorer, then we just stay as cracked as we were before He got here. We can't keep any confidence in Him because we have never trusted Him to put the pieces of our lives back together.

⁎●⁎ evening

···

. . . apart from me you can do nothing. John 15:5

Without Christ I can do absolutely nothing! With Him, I can do *all* things! When Peter and John appeared before the Sanhedrin, Acts 4:13 says, *When they saw the courage of Peter and John and realized they were just unschooled ordinary men, they were astonished and took note of them because they had been with Jesus.* That word "courage" is our same word, "parrhesia," which also means confidence. God-given confidence is not only courage, but competence, and not only competence, but conspicuousness. A human vessel with God confidence displays God at all times. If you're operating out of God confidence, then He is showing in you, because He is causing you to do something you cannot do in your own humanity.

God, help me shake the limitations my mind, and other people put on me. My heart longs to be steadfast in You, confident You work through people like me – the very ones who lack confidence in themselves.

keep your wits about you

 morning

And what I have forgiven – if there was anything to forgive – I have forgiven in the sight of Christ for your sake, in order that Satan might not outwit us. For we are not unaware of his schemes.
2 Corinthians 2:10–11 NIV 1984

All of our sins, past, present and future, went to the cross with Christ. When we think we are unforgiven or when we won't forgive, it can catapult us into a life of severe temptation, things like anger and entitlement. Every time we refuse to forgive, Satan will outwit us and he will have a scheme. There is something he is after, and unforgiveness is the path he will take to get us where he wants us. No matter what depth of hurt you've been through, it is time to forgive.

✴●✴ evening

....

He did not waver at the promise of God through unbelief, but was strengthened in faith, giving glory to God, and being fully convinced that what He had promised He was also able to perform.
Romans 4:20–21 NKJV

You will never walk in faith and not have an invitation to disbelieve God. It can't happen. With every opportunity to believe God, you've got an invitation to disbelieve Him. If we're thinking we're going to have a faith walk without having a wonderful invitation to doubt and fear and disbelief, we've misunderstood our scriptures. But your faith is even more important to Him than your acts of righteousness.

I remind myself again that this is a walk of faith – actually "the good fight of faith." I'm equipped for battle, the Lord is on my side, and *"the life which I now live in the flesh I live by faith in the Son of God, who loved me and gave Himself for me"* **(Galatians 2:20 NKJV).**

DAY 88

wounded hearts must be healed

morning

*My wounds stink and fester because of my foolishness
. . .* Psalm 38:5 ESV

If you have been hurt deeply, you don't want to maintain that wound. When we maintain a wound (broken, hurt heart) we either become victims or victimizers. When a wound festers, it is that much easier for someone else to come along and wound you again. Allow God to get all the way to the root of the wound. To whatever degree you allow Him into that area of your heart, that's the degree of healing you will receive over that wound. Is there a wound that you are just maintaining? Let God completely heal it.

☀ evening

My friends and companions avoid me because of my wounds; my neighbors stay far away. Psalm 38:11

If you can look back over the course of your life and you have ten devastated relationships in your path, something is wrong. Quit looking at everybody else. Take a look at yourself: Were you the only common denominator in those ten relationships? Maybe there is a much greater issue that the Lord wants to heal in your heart; maybe the problem is not the other person, maybe it's you. This is not meant for accusation, it is for the purpose of deep restoration and healing. Ask the Lord to open your eyes to the root of your broken relationships. God wants to restore you.

Create in me a clean heart and a healed heart. Help me to walk in wholeness, Father, so I can be used by You to help bind up the wounded.

love, love, love

 morning

And now these three remain: faith, hope and love. But the greatest of these is love. 1 Corinthians 13:13

Faith expressing itself through love – there is no greater priority as a follower of Christ, just as Paul wrote to the believers in Corinth. Love is the priority. Are there any areas in your life where love has diminished? We can have diminishing love in our marriage, our friendships, towards our church body, or even towards hurting and lost people. A mark of knowing God is to show love. Keep your love for Christ a priority, for He is the One Who maintains our love for others; we cannot maintain it on our own.

● evening

And over all these virtues put on love, which binds them all together in perfect unity. Colossians 3:14

As a child of God, you can't get away from the command to love. "But, I don't want to get hurt again," I sometimes hear. I understand that, but if we are going to love a lot, we might get hurt a lot. It also means we are going to live life! When we give it up on our death bed one of these days, it is not going to be coldness that is going to sustain us. It's going to be the knowledge, not that we did everything right, but that we loved big! We didn't die lonely because there are a whole lot of people around us that we love and who love us. That we loved big . . . not perfectly, but big.

Help me to love big, God. Help me to move toward those I've possibly cut off or pulled away from. May Your love shine big within me.

anywhere, anytime, anyplace!

 morning

Therefore do not throw away your confidence, which has a great reward. For you have need of endurance, so that when you have done the will of God you may receive what is promised. Hebrews 10:35–36 ESV

When we find ourselves intimidated, we need to speak aloud the verses above. Don't just think those words, say them. There is power in words. When your ears literally hear what your mouth is saying. All wisdom and knowledge belong to God, so do not believe that God cannot help you in a certain situation. Anywhere you carry the Spirit of Christ in your vessel is a spiritual place because you walked with the Holy Spirit into that place. The Lord wants to make you profoundly effective. Don't compartmentalize or put limits on where Christ could work through you with His power. Any place you are is a place God wants to work through!

evening

Now when they saw the boldness of Peter and John, and perceived that they were unschooled, ordinary men, they were astonished and they took note that these men had been with Jesus. Acts 4:13

We've gotten confidence confused with pride and arrogance, and many have let the enemy drain them of the confidence and competence we were given in Christ. Confidence and pride are not the same thing. We will never be able to accomplish the will of God in our lives without the kind of confidence that comes from God. If we are living our lives in the confidence He gives, then He is showing up, He is conspicuous in us and He is causing us to do something we cannot do in our own humanity.

My strength is in You, Lord, and every talent I have I dedicate to the purpose that You can use for Your glory. I choose to decrease myself and ask Jesus to be increased and evident in my life.

notes

notes